Help in Understanding Theology

Norman R. DePuy

Help in Understanding Theology

Judson Press ® Valley Forge

Creation
Christ
God
Church
Bible
Holy Spirit

Library of Congress Cataloging in Publication Data

De Puy, Norman R.
  Help in understanding theology.

  1. Theology, Doctrinal—Popular works.   I. Title.
BT77.D397   230   79-20120
ISBN 0-8170-0847-0

To my several congregations,
Osbornville, Hightstown, Moorestown, Ardmore,
and, in particular, Dearborn,
who have been for me the People of God

Contents

INTRODUCTION

You Are Here

One of my favorite therapies is to visit towns and cities in which I have never been before, strolling the streets, looking in the shops, observing the people as they live out their lives. Architecture interests me; the commercial vitality or the lack thereof and the presence or absence of cultural institutions are interesting both in their similarity and in their differences. It is always helpful before you attempt to "case" a town to have an idea of how the town is laid out and where certain points of interest might be; this allows you to enjoy more leisurely its charm and detail and gives you more freedom to observe and absorb.

My aim in this slight study will be to provide the map which will enable us to get our bearings regarding theology, to relax and take in more because we have a sense of what the "town" is like. If necessary we can make notes to remind ourselves to come back and spend more time at a given place. I will move quickly because space is limited, and for most of us the time to read and ponder is also limited. There are splendid works of theology available to any who want to explore in detail. But there is virtue in moving quickly, even as there is still more enjoyment in coming back and savoring certain sights. So we begin. Like those maps we often find with a little circle saying "You Are Here," we will begin where we are—with our own experiences.

Most theological studies are organized like a dictionary, with a heavenly hierarchy serving as the organizing alphabet. They start at the top with God, then move to the Son and then to the Holy Spirit. I don't mean to imply that there is a descending order there, but for whatever reason, that seems to be the traditional order of study. We'll approach things a bit differently. We will talk first about Christ, who is not only the Son but also the Creator in a very real sense. Then we will go to God, who is not only the Father but also the One who shows us our humanity. Then we will consider the Holy Spirit, who is not only whatever he is but also shows us community.

When we talk about creation, we'll try to understand what life is all about and where it is heading. Ordinarily we think of Christ as showing us only what God is about in saving us from our sins. Indeed, that's most significant; but we must not ignore the first verses of John's account of Jesus, nor can we ignore Paul's insistence in several places that in Jesus, the Christ, God was working out his plan which existed even before the world (see Ephesians 1:4-10; 3:1-12). This is important stuff and a good beginning for us.

Then we'll move to God the Father and see what that means for our view of ourselves as human beings. Ordinarily when we think of God, we start with soaring theories and proofs about the Unmoved Mover or some other grand argument. But there is much to be said for understanding ourselves in the light of a God who acts, as he did with Israel. (See discussion on page 38.)

Then we'll consider the Holy Spirit. So often when we talk at length about God as Father and God as Son, we then treat the Spirit as if he were the vapor which exists between the two, or the natural gas which sort of heats and cooks and makes real for us what we think about God the Father and God the Son. But the Holy Spirit is as much an "individual" as the other two "persons" in the Trinity and is just as real as our bones. God's Spirit teaches us what it means to be sociable, about how to get along, or, better, how to love one another as Jesus commands. God's Spirit enables us to love not only those buying something from us or giving us something but our enemies as well. The Spirit is that side of God which tells us about families, lovers, friends, and this crazy thing we call the church, one body made up of many parts. Those parts can't exist apart from one another, as Paul warned the local church in Corinth (see 1 Corinthians 12:12-26).

No one's been in the local church very long without knowing the scandal of a group of odd and often hypocritical people who claim to be the very body of Jesus Christ. Many years ago, when the church was prosperous in spite of itself, John McAfee Brown likened the church to Noah's ark; the only reason the people could stand the stench on the inside was because of the storm on the outside. But that was years ago; since then, a lot of sensitive and sincere people have forsaken the church and decided to take their chances with the storm rather than spend more time in the wasteful, racist, sexist, mindless, wheel-spinning irrelevance which they see the church to be. But is it so? Need it be so?

Why go to church at all? Why think about theology? Can't we be Christians off by ourselves, without the church, watching TV and sending in our contributions to some great "work"? Or to turn the question around and to face in the other direction, how can we possibly live in a rotten world, be honest and real in that world, if we are regular attenders at church where we are taught to behave very differently from the way we behave the other six days of the week?

God in his Spirit creates life both within and without the church, not only in and through Christians but also in and through people everywhere—even those who do their best to resist him, even those cynics who try to live as if this world were all a mistake, turned loose only to run down like a watch.

Do we believe any of this? All of it? Why? Why not? Your answers to these and other questions are "your" gospel, your theology, what you think God is about in this old world of ours. And, obviously, what I will say in these pages is "my gospel." But I, like the apostle Paul (see Romans 1:16), am not ashamed of "my gospel," for it is the same gospel as Paul's and, I dare say, yours. Mentioning a personal pronoun in the same breath with the word "gospel" must strike us as incongruous and perhaps even irreverent. How can the mighty gospel, God's own Good News from on high, be modified by a possessive and earthbound personal pronoun? Can the Good News of the gospel ever be "according to" any human being? Wouldn't such a "gospel" be hopelessly corrupted by human bias and limitations? And yet, remember that the Gospel accounts in the Scriptures are sifted through human minds and the spirits of the Gospel writers.

In our own personal experiences, we, too, have seen Jesus; and what's more, we must make something of it all. We must come to "own" the initial impact which God has made upon us. We must internalize it, digest it, and make it part of our very tissue. We write, as it were, a gospel for our own experience, and the holy gospel must in fact and in life become ours; thus, "my gospel" is the only possible gospel.

In Christian theology, there are no professionals, only degrees of sophistication. We cannot have a claim on the gospel based, as it is, on an experience with the living God without that experience affecting our minds. We have to think about it, and when we do, we have a theology. Theology will always be autobiographical, no matter how careful we might be in trying to do justice to all that

11

others have thought. Frederick Buechner, Christian novelist and theologian, sums it up:

> . . . most theology, like most fiction, is essentially autobiography. Aquinas, Calvin, Barth, Tillich, working out their systems in their own ways in their own language, are all telling us the stories of their lives, and if you press them far enough, even at the most cerebral and forbidding, you find an experience of flesh and blood, a human face smiling or frowning or weeping or covering its eyes before something that happened once . . . maybe no more than a child falling sick, a thunderstorm, a dream, and yet it made . . . a difference which no theology can ever entirely convey or entirely conceal.[1]

We must be reminded, however (and we'll have more to say about this later), that when we do get to thinking about our experience with God, we nevertheless remain persons—creatures—tainted with sin. That must not keep us from thinking, but it does make us continually suspicious of our own opinions. Only God is true and perfect. God gave us perception and minds to use, even if our ideas must remain partial and incomplete. There is no question that we will have a theology. The only question is whether or not it will be good, clear, and meaningful. For us, to be mindless, sloppy, or lazy, or to ignore what good people in other times have thought or felt, is to deny the very faith we claim, the discipleship which promises to God one's mind as well as one's money and energy. No Christian is too dense to increase his or her understanding; no one is so limited in education that he or she does not have strong feelings about God; and no one is incapable of laying out for further speculation his or her thoughts. I hope in this little book to provoke creatively your theology.

As I have already implied, we must always approach the task of theology with humility; our word is never the last one. The first word and the last word belong to the One who is First and Last. Our humility must be true; it must not be the hypocritical modesty which keeps us from thinking, probing, arguing, wrestling with bigger thoughts than we've ever had before. Remember that it will be impossible to have a thought which God has not already had or one so big that God is not wrapped around the outside of it. God can well take care of himself. We can be free to think without the intimidating anxiety that we might create a heresy which will be either a surprise or a threat to God. We can afford to vibrate and resonate to the powerful implications of what happened in Jesus Christ.

[1] Frederick Buechner, *An Alphabet of Grace* (New York: The Seabury Press, Inc., 1970), p. 3.

PART I

Christ, the Clue to Creation

1

Christ, the Clue

In any attempt to work through our understanding of Christian theology, we have to get our minds in hand, as it were. We need a clue. We have been made thinking creatures by God, and being intelligent about the faith is a moral obligation. Our pastors must minister to our minds as well as to our bodies and spirits. But we need to recognize at the outset that though we must think, we must not think too far. By that I mean that we must not assume that we are dealing with problems which are capable of solutions if we just think hard enough. Theology does not deal with problems but, rather, is full of mysteries. There is a clear distinction between the two. A mystery is something which absorbs us, surrounds us, and takes us up into itself. A mystery is something we experience and is beyond the power of our minds to grasp fully. Problems are capable of solutions; mysteries have no solutions. With mystery the most we can expect is a clue. If at any point in working through our theology we get the clear feeling that we understand what we are doing, we must promise ourselves at this early juncture to take another hard look. When we understand completely with our human minds, the chances are very good that we are in error. A proper understanding of Christian theology is the ability to hold a number of things in tension at one and the same time, not reconciling them or smoothing them out to a false consistency.

Such a godly inconsistency is often highly offensive in our time because we have been educated to be "scientific." When TV hucksters want to sell something, they put their actor in a white coat, the symbol of an authority behind the product—an image which leaves little room for doubt. The phrase "doctors recommend" is good enough for us. We are not prone to ask questions about which doctors, how many, where they are coming from, and what the exact nature is of the product they are selling. So brainwashed have we become about the authority of science! To look at our world, to measure, to weigh facts, to organize the facts into a theory is to be applauded by Christian people. But that's not theology. It may be part of a theology, but in theology we are dealing with profound mysteries about God, and we can't allow ourselves to fall into the easily understandable desire to organize things and to work out theories by which we can "prove" God to the satisfaction of any objective observer. A God who can be proven or who can be demonstrated as a theory is not the God with whom we have to deal in the Scriptures, nor is he the God of any other religious faith.

Therefore, it is important to make a promise to ourselves at the outset that if things seem to be clear and consistent, we are probably in trouble. But such humility does not keep us from struggling with our lives, with our experiences, and with a certain revelation which has been given to us just because God is the kind of God he is—a giving, self-revealing God. As we live our lives, questions are thrust upon us whether we are ready for them or not. The days go by, and we have to make a decision about "time" and what it means to grow older, gradually to lose our strength, perhaps even our mental acumen. We have to deal with these life changes. Loved ones are separated from us either because they have matured and left the nest, as it were, or because they are taken by disease and death. Our vocational goals shift; when we are fifty, they are not what they were when we were twenty-eight. Experience changes us and our values have to be shuffled. Nations battle and our sons are called to die for their country. We find traces of meanness and hate in our lives even when we do our best to eliminate all of the "isms" which God finds so abhorrent: racism, sexism, ageism, and all the political "isms." What are we to do? Where is the path? How are we to respond? Where is this whole world of ours going?

These questions are pertinent not just to persons without an education or without the discipline of scientific sophistication. These questions also pertain to the scientist at her microscope, the Ph.D. at her lectern, and the statesman with his finger on the trigger of the neutron bomb.

Jesus, the Clue to Creation

The answer of the Christian faith is that there is but one clue. The answer is the same for all persons regardless of age, sex, or station in life. No matter how complex the problem, no matter how profound it may be, the Clue is in the mystery we call Jesus the Christ.

This is the essential testimony of John's life story of Jesus. We've got to remember that John's Gospel was written well after Jesus had died and had been raised from the dead. It is called "the spiritual Gospel" because it brings an eternal dimension to this man Jesus and sees him as more than a man. Not that the other Gospels see him as less than the Son of God, but John gives us insights which are not in the other Gospels and which are matched only occasionally in their cosmic view by the apostle Paul in some of his letters.

John insists that Jesus is the Clue to creation. We often think of Jesus as Redeemer, which he certainly is, but we have to see also that he is God's sign to us as to what this life of ours is all about.

In John's Gospel story Jesus is referred to as the "Logos." This word carries a mountain of meaning. It is Greek for "word," but it means much more than "word" does in English. In the way it is used in John's Gospel it means the mind, will, and power of God. When God speaks his word, there is no separation of that word, the deed, or the accomplishment. We humans talk and talk and talk, and ofttimes there is little result or consequence to our words. But not so with God. When God speaks a word, the meaning of that word is accomplished by his authority and power. So when John says that Jesus is God's Word, he is not speaking idly about a mere utterance of some kind but, rather, about the purpose and mind of God so that if we want to know what the will of God is for our world, we look to God's Word, Jesus Christ.

John elaborates by saying that Jesus was with God in the original creative process and that nothing in this world has been created apart from Jesus. This is a staggering mystery and can never be understood by our human categories or our human frame of mind. How can this peasant who was born of humble parents, who walked in a real country in a real point in history also be the mind of God in creation which lies beyond all recorded history? There is no answer, just the statement of John's Gospel. We must investigate until our hearts are content or our minds satisfied—or frustrated—as the case may be. But we begin and end with the Clue given to us by God through John.

What kind of a God is it with whom we have to do? The Clue is Jesus. Where is this creation heading? The answer is in Jesus. How do we know what is right and wrong? The answer, again, is Jesus.

If we are confused about what the world is saying to us about power, if the race seems to be to the swift and deference to the beautiful, what does God's Clue say? If our children are taken away by disease and death in the prime of their brief lives, what does "brief" mean? What does it mean that we are all running out of time, with dreams unfulfilled and visions tarnished? What does Jesus have to say about longevity? About the use of time, about attitudes toward the past or the future? Is nature evil? Is nature working against us or for us? Where are our human roots? Are they in history forever, or is there some other dimension, different and "above," which is able to break in upon us?

Jesus has been called "the near side of God." He is a Clue which, if we can't understand, we can at least grasp. He was a man who was kissed and embraced. He was a man who spoke and who taught. He was a person who loved and elicited love. He touched people who needed to be touched by God. He had certain attitudes toward the lilies of the field and the birds of the air (see Matthew 6:28; 8:20). Those attitudes are God's attitudes. He is our Clue on earth.

John, as well as the apostle Paul, insists that Jesus was the Lamb slain before the foundation of the world (see John 17:24; Ephesians 1:3-10). The testimony of John and Paul are the same: this Christ was preexistent—he was even before existence.

He brings, therefore, to our lives the intimations of eternity, shadows and vibrations from another world beyond time. He is arbitrary and taught with authority as no one else had ever taught before him. He contained in himself the very authority of God's own word, God's own power.

The people of Israel in Jesus' time were like all of us. They wanted to push the great day of reckoning, the day when God's word would clearly be known among them, off into the future. But John would not allow that evasion. He wrote his Gospel story so people would know that this Jesus was indeed their day of reckoning, the Word and the Clue they wanted from God. They could not put it off nor could they dodge and avoid the issue. They were facing God's Clue in Jesus Christ, and they had to respond.

Jesus, the Personal Clue

Love can be brutal. We believe that God is love, and, therefore, the core of all of life and the universe is love. But love unanswered can be a chastisement. When love won't let you go; when it pursues you; when it confronts you with any word which you don't want to hear particularly, which could cause you to leave all and follow, which could make you see the value of giving away your money and life itself, which heals beggars when they've become quite accustomed (thank you) to begging; it can be disconcerting at best and downright threatening at worst.

So we're not talking about sentimentality here—not a silly little proposition presented to us by God, but a Word which was alive. If not understandable, at least graspable; a word which if not moderate was commanding and had all the authority of a king about it.

The nature of the Clue itself is a clue. God could have given us a clue which was written on tables of stone, even as the clue was which he gave to Moses. But he didn't. His word did not come to us in a book or in a philosopher's argument. It came in a person, who had to be known personally. It was a Word which could be seen with the eye, heard with the ear, and touched with the fingers. Though it was a Word which the mind needed to grapple with, searching brown, Jewish eyes replaced the coldness of stone tablets. Thus, because the Clue itself is a person, because the word we have from God needs to be taken into our personality, we see that God is love and can only be known in love.

Love never rapes. It expresses itself and waits. It pursues but it does not violate. Thus, the personal Clue is a clue which can only be taken into our being and into our awareness by love. This is why we can, for reasons which are not at all efficient from our point of view, reject the Clue. I am sure that if we were God, we would strike dead anyone who would turn his or her back on the central Clue to all existence. Such stupidity and idiocy! But because God is love, he gives us a Clue which is love personified and which waits for our response.

The God of love pursues, woos, treats us with great tenderness even when he could destroy us if such were his intention. So the Clue we have in Christ gives us a clue to the intention of God; he is lover and not tyrant or dictator.

This tells us something about the world in which we live. Nature can be harsh and inexorable. Floodwaters will drown us; fire will burn us. Nature has no conscience and can't make decisions. Arbitrary things visit us and make us wonder whether or not God is, indeed, love. When children are killed in a fire or innocent people are murdered, what is the clue here? What is the clue when hardworking and earnest people of faith are stricken with cancer or coronary disease? How can love be the clue to our understanding of all of this?

Our Clue, Jesus, was not himself free of suffering. Again, God took on human flesh, became a man who in all ways is as we are. He was not free from suffering. He was tempted, he was tried, and he felt pain. He became tired; he became short-tempered with the religious sham of his day; he wept over those who would not accept the Clue, over those who preferred their own manufactured faith rather than faith in the living God. God became human. Humanity is thus blessed by God. God is interested in persons. He became a person. Therefore, personhood must be primary, a clue to understanding ourselves. Suffering, evil, and all the things in nature which we can't understand cannot be allowed to discourage us or dishearten us. We have had a stamp placed on us by God's Word. Because he became human, we can rejoice in being human. As he partook of his own creation in the man Jesus, who was also part of that original creative force, then his creation must have about it a goodness, certainly a hope. So we have a Clue to the meaning of our world and how we fit into it.

The Clue, Full of Authority and Power

Jesus, the Word of God, had an authority over nature. He dominated the storm, walked on the water, called out demons, and healed people. He had power over the loaves and fishes. We can't begin to understand any scientific treatment of these episodes because they were not written with any regard for measurement or for modern science. They are trying to tell us of a truth far more profound than that of cells, molecules, and atoms. They are telling us about authority over evil and disease in nature. Though we suffer, we have a Clue which has all the authority of the Creator himself over the creation. This investing of authority is a clue to our attitude toward nature (see Genesis 1:26).

Eventually, in "the fulness of the time" (Galatians 4:4) the Clue came in Christ. It does not, fascinatingly enough, contradict those ancient creation poems in the first three chapters of Genesis.

Jesus moved out from the confines of religious organization to the streets and the roads. He mingled with the common people, and he blessed them without regard for their religious station. This is a clue to what authority means and how it is to be distributed to persons. If Jesus had no regard for religious hierarchy, then what does that say to us about God's will for the church? If Jesus said that the last shall be first and the first shall be last (see Mark 9:35), what is he saying to us about power and prestige?

If Jesus, with all the authority of God in creating the whole world, stands dumb before his accusers and warns us against the use of power, if the Word of God in Jesus insists that we are not to live by the sword, what of our bombs and our armies? If God stands dumb before his accusers, then what is his word to us about retaliation?

If God gives us a word which says that there is to be no such thing as segregation, how shall we define neighbors? If even the hated Samaritan is our neighbor, what is God saying to us about the nature of clubs and exclusive attitudes in neighborhoods about "proper addresses" as well as other forms of social exclusion, not the least of which is racial segregation?

When John talks about Jesus the way he does in the first few verses of his Gospel account, he's talking not about some philosophical category or some vague intellectual argument but, rather, about power in action—the action of healing, walking on water, feeding the people, raising the dead. It is the resurrection in action by which God's power transmutes and changes the physical. When the sun grew dark in the crucifixion, could it be that it was deferring to a brighter light, not figuratively but literally?

When the veil of the temple was rent at the time of Jesus' death, when the Clue was crucified, all empty rooms and hollow centers in history and time were filled with the power of God. Into the dark recess where only the high priest had gone once a year now suddenly flooded light so that all could see that God was not a God confined to darkness, but the God of sun and the wind and the air. It was an open and royal invitation to all creation to see what is at the core of the universe and of being.

We're not dealing with hyperbole or oriental exaggerations in these early verses of John's Gospel story. We are talking physics and chemistry. We're talking about the power of the atom, the power of photosynthesis by which plants make food, the power of the rising sun and the turning of the earth. John is insisting that the force of gravity is in some way related to this mysterious, humble Galilean. The meaning of an apple falling on Newton's head does not happen without the catalytic Christ. Impossible to understand but important to believe.

It means that the root of life is the same power which healed and conquered the storm. When Jesus said that the way to save one's life was to lose it, that love is eternal though the body rots, he was talking about physics and medicine as well as theology.

Who knows the precise distinction between the physical and the social or how one influences the other? What is the relationship of the body to the mind, of emotional stress to cancer or any other disease? What is the relationship of spirit to primal energy? Bacteria is only an intermediate explanation of disease. What is the relationship of the sun to the resurrection of the dead? The Clue to defining is not to be found in abstract philosophy, or careful measurement, but by focus on God in Jesus of Nazareth. If we talk of genius or intelligence, foreign policy or military power, industrialization or the stewardship of national resources on this spaceship earth, we must discuss them in those ethical values projected in the person of Jesus, consistent with the mystery of his control over persons and over nature.

The research now going on in biofeedback, for instance, only confirms what many suspected for a long time—that perhaps in one way or another all history, all bodily functions are controlled through the will. The human mind can change the condition of bodily functions heretofore assumed to be autonomous and beyond the control of consciousness. Imagine, then, what could happen when God's will is merged with our will!

What, then, is the place of gentleness, of profound regard for nature, of Christ, of stewardship, of peace and development of goodwill among persons? The Prince of Peace, the One who places persons above principles and who saw that his confidence in God was enough power to take care of the morrow, is the Clue. He could afford to emulate the confidence of the lily of the field and to trust God for the conquest over death. This must not be lost on us.

None of this should be too clear, as we said at the outset. We've talked about staggering concepts, and no legitimate theology can minimize the complexity or the contradictions. They are beyond understanding. But we have in Jesus Christ a mystery which absorbs us into itself. The only assertion we can make is the faithful assertion that the Clue to all creation is in the Word of God which is in Jesus.

Too often the church has been willing to allow itself to be put down for lack of sophistication and relegated to the back row by intellectuals and people committed to other values. But when we insist that the Logos of God, his mind and his word, which are one and the same, has come to us in Jesus, we are of all persons most sophisticated, most able to see, to understand, to be understood, and to call upon the power which is at the core of all creation. The world does not falter for lack of ideas but for lack of power, for lack of authority. We have an authoritative and powerful Clue.

We have no easy answers, but we must see that in Jesus Christ we have a Clue which enables us to look at the typhoon, the earthquake, and the setting of the stars in the heavens, at disease and human mistakes and to say we know something of what God intends.

The riddle of the universe is to be seen not in vague speculation about power and prestige but, rather, in the One who came riding upon an ass into the capital city.

2

Christ, the Redeemer

But God is saying even more to us in Christ than we have thus far considered. He not only shows us a clue to the world around us, but he also *does* something in Christ. He becomes like us in order to save us.

Our Need for Redemption

There may well be in any open and honest discussion of theology a debate as to why we need saving. Humans are proud (which is the root of our problem), and we don't like the idea that we are not whole, that we are lost, that we are confused, or that we need redeeming like so many Green Stamps. It is a humiliating suggestion.

There are those who argue quite logically and cogently that if persons had just a bit more education, they would be okay. That our cities would not be in a mess if we just planned more carefully. That nations would not slaughter one another if sensible people armed with goodwill and information would sit down in a room and discuss things calmly and coolly without charges and countercharges. That the hatred we feel for people who are different from ourselves can be resolved by practices of goodwill, such as Brotherhood Week.

Still others feel that though we do have severe problems, these problems can be solved by more earnest application of science and technology. (Christians do have to be honest and grant to scientists that they might well someday find an answer to human nature, to disease, to the cruelty and meanness which characterize human behavior and which literally shout at us from the six o'clock news. There is no way we can disprove the scientist's faith and hope for a solution, even if thus far history judges science rather harshly.)

And still others would argue that if we can go through a process of analysis and thinking about the various pressures to which we have been subjected in the past and in our childhood, we will find a way out of the darkness. If our childhood experiences can be sorted out and we can look at them coolly and sensibly, we will find peace of mind and power to act as we should.

And yet still others think it's all a matter of chemistry; if we can find the right chemical balance in the human brain, we will have a clue to our insanity, to the barbarism, and to the self-destructive lack of initiative found in so many. Nothing is more widespread in our society than the malaise we call depression, be it acute or chronic. If we could just find the right pill, we will have found the answer, says the psychological society.

Medical science and technology are moving at such a rapid rate these days that there is talk of cloning and the generation of life in test tubes. We are already able to start a fetus with the sperm and the egg of human beings by placing both of them in a test-tube culture. What next? We transplant organs, even experimenting with transplanting organs from animals to humans. Surely this will be the answer, moderns argue, to those who are crippled in one way or another.

For still others the clue to remedying the rotten behavior of people is money or in economics. If a proper distribution of goods could be achieved through five-year plans or twenty-year plans or however many years, then all would be well and heaven would come on earth. The culprit is greed, say these people. We call them socialists or communists. Capitalism assumes selfishness as part of the human condition; gratification will provide the saving motivation.

But whether the answer be in more education, in the distribution of goods, in chemistry or psychological analysis, almost anyone who has any sense at all will admit that ours, indeed, is a sad and sorry world full of misery and heartache, replete with frustrated potential and unfulfilled promises.

Christians are no different. Christians begin with an honest assessment of this world. Biblical writers do not shy away from evil or moral wickedness. They face it full on, and they proclaim answers— or better, the Answer.

24

Jesus Christ, the Answer to the Problem of Evil in Our World

The supreme answer for the Christian is Jesus Christ as

Redeemer. In him, in some strange way God offered himself to us for our salvation.

The church has argued through the centuries about how this "at-one-ment" (atonement) could have taken place. Was it necessary because God is perfect and just and cannot tolerate imperfection, thereby "buying" our perfection with his own? Perhaps that element is present.

But all that we can know with certainty is that this one called Jesus, whom faith named the Son of God, died on a cross for love of people and that somehow God himself was in that death.

If we attempt, as heretics have often done (and remember that heretics are earnest Christians struggling with mighty truths), to separate Jesus from God or God from Jesus; if we try to say that Jesus was only man, or only seemed to be God, we are in real trouble. If Jesus is in any way less than God, then his death was the death of a mere man, and Jesus becomes a martyr alongside the many great martyrs through history. We must hang onto the mystery of God doing for us what is needed. He is both the giver and the gift. A most difficult problem. But remember—we enter into mysteries; we do not solve problems.

At the same time, it is critically important that Jesus be completely human. He needs to have glands, hunger, thirst, sexual urges. He needs to be limited in his ability to be in more than one place at a time; it is only after he received his new body, after the resurrection, that he was able to move about without regard for doors and walls and space. He took on definite human limitations, and it is imperative that we never lose sight of that point. Anything less than full and complete humanity for Jesus leaves us with a Redeemer who was not as we are, who did not understand our sin, and who did not know anything of the cost of forgiving it.

We must hold to both his being God and man. In ways beyond our ability to describe, though Matthew and Luke try describing it in their accounts of the virgin birth, God enters into flesh; and indeed it was God's own power and presence which were in this stranger of Galilee called Jesus. No matter how much we are tempted to think of Jesus only as a teacher, we cannot handle the New Testament evidence without recognizing that millions have considered him to be the Christ, the Son of God, the Chosen One, Lord, the One with the power—as we saw in the first chapter—to be the very Clue to God's heart and mind.

Thus, the trinitarian truth remains though we may not find much value in the old wrestling with the concept of the Trinity. Such wrestling was important in the past, but not in our day. What must be retained is the essential truth that God is known to us in history as Father, he is known in Jesus, and he is experienced as Spirit. You can't take any of these away without being in great difficulty. The councils of the church and all of the great creeds which have tried to wrestle with these issues have come up with the same basic assertion, simple and yet ever so complex: that God was in Christ reconciling the world unto himself, in every age, through his Spirit.

In the most extreme evidence of his love, his unwillingness to let us fall from his hand, God allowed his Son, with echoes of Abraham and Isaac, to be sacrificed for our sakes. What Abraham as mere man did not have to do, sacrifice his only son, God in Christ did because he so loved us. Love cannot be pushed any farther than it was pushed in the cross. There is nothing more to be said; nothing less can be said.

Of course, the question arises as to why God would do this. And in our pride we have wrestled, again through the centuries, with all sorts of logical answers.

Some have said because God was holy and required a perfect sacrifice. But this makes God an Oriental despot, which the warm relationship of Jesus to his heavenly Father belies.

Others have said that humankind needs an example of love. Well, Jesus' life and death were certainly that. But Christ was more than an example. Any of us could die rushing into a burning building to save a child and thereby be a great example of heroism, love, and commitment. But there was more than that on the lonely Hill.

The testimony of the church and the Scriptures is that God loves us to the utmost extreme. There is nothing that we can do, including spitting on his love and denying his Lover, which will keep him from loving us. The lowest and most contemptible activity of his own creatures—the murdering of his love—was not allowed to be the last word. That humiliation on Calvary, that exhaustion of all human morality was the devil's last gasp and the last arrow in his quiver.

But that arrow did not bounce off God as if he were a comic book superman. It penetrated his heart; because he is a God of love and not just of muscle, he took the arrow of human frailty, the limitations of his own creation, and absorbed the fatal effects. It cost him a great deal. We are not speaking here of play acting, nor are we making light of the thunderous shaking of the ground during those hours when he hung on the cross. All creation was being redeemed, including nature.

All human bargains and deals, big and little, are done away with by this extravagant act of God's pursuit and love. No longer can we do good little things in order to save ourselves. Such good little things, notes Paul, called the law are indeed admirable, but they are not adequate and, therefore, they kill. "Who will deliver me," said Paul, "from mere good works?" "I do good works and I still do not feel at home in the world, at peace with God, or able to love my enemy or my neighbor. I need more, I need God, I need God's power, I need some evidence of God's presence with me. I need God to deliver me." Paul said, "The things I want to do I don't do, and the things I don't want to do I do. Oh, how shall I get out of this predicament?" (See Romans 7:19, 24.) The answer was Christ, because in Christ God himself was providing the way and the power.

In our day and age we speak with a great deal of anxiety and concern about humanity being obliterated from the earth. What does life count for? Why should we be kind? Why should we make the effort to love? Why should we even relate to our children when they reject what we stand for? The world seems to be coming unglued. It is full of sin and corruption. Such glowering chaos generates in us a sense of impotence and anxiety if not outright fear and panic.

The signs of God's own intervention in the world on our behalf change the picture. In spite of corruption and devastation, there emerges from us a great flood of sympathy and empathy instead of the fear and despair we would logically expect. Our Maker has been gracious. How can we be less so? When we are released from prison, from a death sentence, the natural emotion is one of gratitude. We suddenly find ourselves feeling grateful toward the world and toward others. This is precisely what happens to us when we come to an awareness of a Redeemer who sets us free, smashes our prison houses, and forgives us all of the errors and the stumblings of our past lives in order to guide our steps in the future as well as the present. Such a response is called faith. The related attitude is called forgiveness.

We still, like those foolish Galatians that Paul railed against, want to go back and rebuild our prison cells. Out of the very rubble we try to build new cells rather than use the stones to build new bridges to peace and fellowship with others. Out of sheer perversity we often turn from freedom and light, yearn for "three squares a day" in prison in Egypt, turning away from the Promised Land.

Many feel that a devil and demonic forces exist which make us behave in such a manner, turning our backs on grace and preferring darkness to light. Certainly the Scriptures teach that there is a great battle between God and evil going on and that we are pushed and pulled in this battle. The battle rages; one side has the offensive and then the other. But no offensive can be greater than that which was mounted by evil against Jesus Christ, an offensive which crumbled even as its perpetrators crowed about their victory.

We strut about with our pretentions. We gather our money, our accomplishments, and our academic degrees. We display our titles and wear the proper labels. We live in "good" neighborhoods and make statements of prestige with our clothes and our cars. We carefully wash our hands and faces, use a deodorant which will never let us down, and feel that, indeed, we have become respectable. But no such human superficiality is adequate to the real redemption we need. A redemption which is going to make us so grateful for the forgiveness we have that we will forgive others, even our enemies; a redemption which gives a liberty so great that we will feel pain as long as others are in chains; a redemption which bestows a sense of peace from God so blessed that it causes us to pine for those who do not have it, is what is required to put our sins to rout.

And only a Jesus who is also the Christ, only a peasant who was somehow also God the Father and God the Spirit, is adequate for the task. Any less a faith will lead us astray. Even though we confess in our praise and our worship that we don't understand this glorious thing that has happened to us, we accept it for our salvation. We don't have to understand it to believe it.

3

Christ, the Hope

The early church in Egypt, Rome, and Carthage practiced the striking custom of giving to converts at their first Communion, in addition to bread and wine, a cup of milk and honey. It symbolized the heavenly food of which they would partake in the coming kingdom of God. It was a foretaste of heaven.

No less happened to us in Jesus Christ. We have the bread and the wine. We have the fruit of the grape and the crushed wheat, the blood and the broken body. We have our struggles in this life and we've talked of our redemption in Christ. But there is more to our faith than rejoicing in the past. The milk and honey of the future promised land must be a part of our thinking. We have a blessed Hope.

Christ, Our Down Payment of Heaven

All human beings are carried forward by time, ready or not. There is no greater mystery. Augustine, the great leader in the early church, said, in effect, that he understood "time" perfectly until someone asked him to explain it. We talk of a "present," but by the "time" the words are out of our mouths, it has become the "past." Another philosopher noted that though we live forward, we understand backward. We are carried forward into the future even if we feel unprepared. There is no stopping time. We talk of buying time and killing time and having time on our hands, but those are inaccurate figures of speech. What we are killing and what we are buying and what we have on our hands is ourselves. Time, like "Old

Man River," just rolls along and carries us with it.

The question before the person who is trying to think theologically is not whether time exists or whether or not it is good. The question is, What does it mean and where are we going? The question is one of purpose and direction.

Here, again, Christ is the answer. In Christ we have, according to the apostle Paul, a down payment of heaven. We have an interruption of God and his quality of life into our quality of life, eternity into time.

It is a serious mistake to think of eternity and everlasting as having the same meaning. Eternity might be everlasting, but everlasting is not necessarily eternal. Eternity is a quality of life, just as we talk of people leading privileged lives as "quality folk." Eternity is the highest quality; it does not necessarily have anything to do with one year set cheek by jowl with another. I like to think of eternity as surrounding time. I think of time as a string with a beginning and an ending, but all around the string, if I could suspend it in air, would be eternity. This is a weak analogy which breaks down as all analogies do. We are born and we die. The world changes. The stratification of rock and the course of the glaciers give us clear indication that there is change and movement, a going from one point to another, over a period of time. And as we are borne along, great questions are raised as to our destination and path. We know that God has intervened in history and has pronounced himself King. We talk of the kingdom of God in Jesus Christ. We look backward two thousand years and note that the kingdom was thus established. But we must do more than look back into the time when Jesus lived.

It's not only the past which concerns God. The Christian faith claims no less than that the future can be remembered. That sounds like a contradiction, and obviously by the dictionary's cramped definition, it is. But that is the claim of the gospel nevertheless.

Somehow that kingdom which was established two thousand years ago was established not only then but forever. It was established not only in that particular time but also in eternity. Eternity which has no beginning or ending and which surrounds the "string," as it were, is as much a part of the future as it was of the past. It is always with us, unchanging, and, unlike time, without an end. It is much more than forever.

Eschatology is a big word, but it is a word we should all learn. It has to do with more than the "end times" or the last things. It is a notion peculiar to Christian thinking which indicates that God deals not only with what's at the end of time but also with what is around time, namely, eternity. What is God saying to us about our destiny? Can our beginnings have any connections to our endings?

The fact that we have been redeemed at some point in time is no indication by itself that we shall be kept, or that we shall arrive safely at our destination. Eschatology is the Christian affirmation that indeed in Jesus Christ we were saved, we are being saved, and that one day we shall be completely saved. To neglect any of these three tenses is to miss the scope of God's plan of salvation.

When we turn toward God and confess in faith that indeed God was in Christ as our Savior and Lord, we continue through history. We are changed and yet we remain the same. We have continued with our diseases, our heartaches, and with our confusions. Being saved at some point in the past has not delivered us from the ravages of time. Some of us have had radical changes in our lives; all of us feel changed in some way. Turned about, reorganized, and redirected. But we have also realized that there is a wilderness in which we are wandering and that the manna, unlike the milk and honey of the Promised Land, will last only for the day. We are still dependent upon God's mercy and grace completely and finally and perfectly to deliver us some day. We are not yet complete, though we shall one day be.

The Blessed Hope: God's Answer to Our Death

Of course, for most of us the end of time will be marked by our death. We do our best sometimes with artificial grass at our gravesides, embalming, and other procedures to minimize death. It is humanly understandable because death is indeed ugly. It is a robber and a marauder. We feel it creeping upon us if it doesn't strike us suddenly. It is the last enemy, as the apostle Paul calls it. There is nothing more definite, nothing more threatening to our dignity and to our very lives than death.

Even if we feel redeemed and mightily liberated, even if we were hungry and are now satisfied, even if we were forsaken and now feel loved and accepted, we know that death still stands before us to rob us of our glory and our prize. Unless there is something in the plan of salvation which includes time, blesses time, redeems time, and gives us a time which is not a harbinger of deterioration and death, we are of all persons most miserable.

The answer given to us in Jesus Christ is called the blessed hope. That is the belief that in Christ God was active and that after Christ returned to full eternal fellowship with the Father, whatever that means, a Comforter was given. The word needs to be divided for our modern minds; "com" means "with," and "forte" means "strength."

The Holy Spirit, of which we shall say more later in terms of the church, has been given to us not as a sentimental, wishy-washy feeling. It is "with strength" that God has come to us in the Spirit, to be with us in power, the power of God the Father and God the Son. The Holy Spirit of promise cannot be minimized or made into some kind of an interspace between the Father and Son. The Spirit must have the same personhood as they and be thought of as having personality even as we have personality. This Spirit, then, is with us and bears us up until such time as we die and are face to face with the full measure of that eternity of which we've had a down payment in Jesus Christ.

This has radical meaning for our present deeds and our actions. The future casts a shadow backward into the present. Many of us will never be famous. We'll never receive the applause of the world or its prizes and plaudits. We'll not have college dormitories named after us because we have never made money to give as a memorial. We'll not have any monuments built to us because we've never fought in great wars or been famous military heroes. We'll never get to be glamorous movie stars impressing our feet or some other part of our anatomy in wet cement for all posterity.

The world is quick to tell us, therefore, that we are unimportant, that our actions, thoughts, and feelings are not nearly as significant as those which cram the pages of the fan magazines. But the Christian hope says otherwise. Because we are "otherworldly," because we believe that our perfection lies elsewhere, and that our destiny is elsewhere, because we believe that that "elsewhere" has interrupted our history, we can believe that our thoughts, feelings, and actions are registered not by the world's record books but, rather, by eternal record books. Our roots are not in time but in eternity; as time carries us forward, we are nevertheless marking our time in eternity, a registration which is timeless.

We do not grow older in God's eyes. We mature toward that complete newness which John speaks of in that remarkable book of Revelation; we'll have a new city and a new name, and that name will be written on a white stone which is the mark of conquest and victory. So the older we get, the closer we get to newness, to a new body, to new life. This is contrary to the world's hope, a world which has no ingredient comparable to what we call eschatology.

Many Christians are very much concerned about the details of the Second Coming of Christ. They work out intricate patterns and charts, most of them based either on the Book of Daniel or the book of Revelation. We'll talk a bit about these books when we talk about the authority of Scriptures, but for now let us say that whatever the New Testament teaches about the Second Coming of Christ, the essential meaning is the victory of God and the consummation of everything in Christ, including time. There will be no sequence. The consummation which will be in the Second Advent, the second showing of God's power—even as the first was in "a little baby thing which made a mother cry"—shall come in glory and power. There will be nothing worthwhile "after" that. There will be nothing else to happen. The point of the book of Revelation is that the victory shall be God's. Revelation is not a calendar; it's a proclamation of conquest. It is not concerned about time; it defeats time. It is a message to bedraggled and persecuted Christians that they should not allow time and space and history to wear them down because their citizenship is to be made complete in another dimension— heaven, eternity, the perfect presence of God.

Most future speculations can be labeled, at least by the cynical, as wishful thinking, as projections of one's desires and dreams. Who can contradict such fantasies? The answer, of course, is no one. But for the Christian it is not merely a projection of need or fantasy; it is looking back to what God proclaimed in the "now" of the New Testament times so that the "then" of our future becomes one and the same with it under the lordship of Jesus Christ, God's Clue, God's redemption, and God's gift of hope.

PART II

God, the Savior

4

Honest Abraham

We come now in our theological pilgrimage to some consideration of God, as Christians have traditionally said, "God the Father." The fatherhood of God is implied, of course, in creation and is given a strong impetus in Jesus, God's Clue to his own nature. Further, we are also given the Spirit which makes us feel like sons and daughters, able to call God "Abba," or "Daddy."

But there is that aspect of God which must be considered by and of itself by anyone concerned with theology, leaving aside for the moment the clue we have in Jesus Christ. We have to be fair with people who have not accepted the Clue or even heard about it. Christians should be willing to admit that in a sense God is greater than the Clue. That sounds like heresy, but it's one of those mysteries with which we have to deal. We have a Clue in Jesus Christ whom we have called Lord and God, but there is also the need to understand God as greater than any of God's manifestations to creation.

After all, God was known by those faithful people in the Old Testament, without whom we Christians would not enjoy the knowledge we have in the One we call Lord, who was very much a product of the Old Testament. It is important that we think of God as God, God beyond Jesus, and beyond all God's signs to us creatures. This is not to suggest that Jesus was not God in some mysterious way, but it is to say that there is a sovereignty and a presence which we must deal with apart from Jesus. The really odd thing about any consideration of the being of God is that we learn more about ourselves than we do about God. We are made whole. We are saved. God always remains a mystery, even though we do our best to make God manageable to human intelligence.

In our attempts to understand God, we think in terms of what we have experienced in our lives and in our cultures. In our culture we have thought of the man as having the dominant role—as father in the family, priest in religion, king in the nation. Therefore, when we have thought of God as Creator, Ruler of the universe, supreme Sovereign, we have thought of a male being. In recent years, we have come to realize that there is no reason other than cultural conditioning for placing the male in the dominant role in society. In this light, many have begun to rethink their understanding of God. Even in the Bible there are references to feminine and maternal characteristics in God. In the mystery of God, maleness and femaleness may be combined in a being beyond any way that we, in our limited ways, can imagine. For we continue to think of God in terms of our own experiences.

For instance, when we look to the Old Testament and the experience of the ancient Jews, we find a God who acts in history, on real people in real situations, and these people are changed. They are saved as it were; they are made whole as they respond in allegiance to this God who chooses them to be his own but only so that they can be a blessing to the whole world. Without their calling, the Jews are no special people at all.

Our Need for Faith in God

There is in all humanity the feeling of contingency. That is to say, just by being human we are dependent. We are dependent upon something. It's not always clear that we are dependent on one thing rather than another. Often we build a system of dependencies rather than recognize our one great true dependency. Our system of values works itself out in our lives in various ways, some quite logical and consistent, at other times emotionally with all sorts of jiggles and flip-flops when we are under life's pressure. No human being is independent; we cannot be independent precisely because we are all a part of creation; no human being can be *The* Creator; one can be only an image or shadow of the Creator.

As for the biblical concept of God, there is a radical necessity to eliminate all other gods. I haven't taken much space for these other possibilities, but it is obvious that if a person depends ultimately on one's education, that person has made it a god. If a person believes in magic, he or she has made it a god. And it is most important to realize that we can be no more than what we depend upon. In the Scripture dependence is not tolerated except where God is the object. Thus, true humanness means true dependence on the true God. All other gods are false; all other dependencies will ultimately destroy us.

Our sinful human nature being what it is, we tend to put faith in all sorts of things. If we are unable to sort out all of these other dependencies, we shall never understand what the Christian faith is talking about when it talks of the God of Scripture.

If we are able to bring ourselves to believe in any other gods, we probably should. And we probably will. All true faith must be rooted in doubt. If there is proof, there is no need for faith. Faith easily arrived at will never weather life's crunches and crises. Whatever we believe about God, we need to be real and honest about it and believe in the bad times as well as the good. Faith must be a truly last resort, never a glib answer to life-threatening complexities and troubles. Such faith is dependency in an inadequate God. If we think about it for a moment, we will find that those who seem to have the most trouble are often those who also have the strongest faith. This is not to say that faith comes as a reward for trouble, but it is an interesting thing upon which to speculate. God is God regardless.

Faith in the true God must be rooted deeply and must arise after every other belief has been tried and found wanting. Faith itself needs careful and critical thought.

Some things we call faith are merely dumb resignation, abiding by laws which everyone accepts. We stop at red lights and have "faith" that others will do the same. We may be conservative and edgy about intersections; but if we did not have "faith" in the traffic light, we would never cross such an intersection and would probably end up being "rear-ended." Those behind us will have "faith" in the "faith" of others and will assume that a green light means it is safe to go. Therefore, we must have "faith" as well; we move along with the traffic.

We have so-called "faith" in the captains of our jet airliners, the police officers on patrol, the judges on the bench, and the congressmen in Washington. Although occasionally betrayed, we must have faith in order for society to survive. We live by faith—all sorts of faith and all sorts of values. There is no avoiding faith. But just because faith is as essential to the human spirit as air is to the lungs, we need to be careful what faiths we hold just as we should be concerned about the quality of air which we breathe.

At this point we are human in the best sense of that word. Animals are inhuman, not because they walk on all fours, not because they have nothing physiologically in common with people, but because they choose only by instinct. Animals are inhuman because they behave by instinct. People, for better or worse, choose how they will behave, and they choose on the basis of their faith, or more accurately, faiths. Just as we are what we eat, we are also what we believe. That in which we place our trust will shape our very being as well as the way we live.

We must be honest about faith in God; faith in the living God of the Bible does not come easily. Human beings will project all sorts of foolish faiths into the air, call them "God," and then believe them. Our human needs are many times painful. We will kid ourselves forever if our own little manufactured faith gives us even some small relief. That is, some of us will. There are always in every age those who will not be easily deceived and who at great cost give themselves to God, to a large faith, the faith which saves and defines.

Such persons are honest about their feelings and their needs to the point that they doubt easy answers and questionable gods. They are often the seekers and the searchers, sometimes persons who try our patience. No doubt such doubters often forget to doubt their doubts, and falling into the morass of pessimism and whining cynicism, they flail about. But the ones who will not accept the little do-it-yourself homemade gods are those ripe to hear the word of the living God.

In a sense, then, a God who is greater than all our human theories will be worshiped only by those who have reached the end of their rope. Not necessarily desperate (though some theologians would insist on that) but certainly at the end of their human resources, in terms of meeting the deep desires of their hearts. They recognize their dependency upon God.

The true God is the refiner and definer of our dependence on him and thereby shows us what it means to be a person even as he shows himself as true God.

So we proceed in our study with some of these tough, honest people who would not accept easy faiths, whose doubts made them open to the One who was finally irresistible, the One worthy of supreme trust.

Shaped by Our Call

Abraham of old was a person defined and shaped by his great need for faith. God, at least in the Bible, seldom calls or speaks to shriveled people. They may be large only in their sinfulness, like the apostle Paul, but large nevertheless. After meeting God, they change direction and grow; but the large, generous quality remains, as well as the large doubts which led to the large God. Abraham is the model for faith to which Jesus, Paul, and the writer of the New Testament book called Hebrews return. The apostle Paul was anxious to point out that it was precisely Abraham's doubt and openness of spirit which enabled him to be the father of the Jews (see Romans 4:18), rather than any dependence on his part on little laws so easy to see and measure.

Therefore, it is striking that when God made his move, according to his purpose for the world, Abraham responded without question. There comes a point where questions are out of order when dealing with the living God, the God before all other gods, the only One who will not in the last analysis tolerate question. So Abraham, noted for his openness, did the absurd thing: he left his homeland—no easy thing in those times when your clan was your salvation. He was willing to kill his last chance, as it were, even his son, Isaac. Sarah laughed when she heard the news that she would become pregnant. Such an absurd notion; they were to have a last chance. She was to bear a child. They did have a child, and his name was Isaac, "the one who laughs." Abraham raised a knife in blind obedience, not because he was unthinking and coldhearted, but, rather, because he was too caring and passionate to turn against the God who was not to rest on Abraham's private domestic altar but in his heart, a God who dominated and who suffered no rival. Such a God was terrible and awful but was, indeed, God in the deepest sense of the word. Such utter dependency puts all other dependencies to shame. Oddly, it also produces a singular honesty, an integrity (together) integrated. Our honesty is shaped by our faith in God. We are what we believe.

It is interesting that this early recorded response to the living God, the response of Abraham, was not based on any philosophical doctrine, any argument, any great proof. We recognize the existence of philosophical proofs of God, which have been rehearsed by sophomores through the ages. Some feel that there is a God because the world seems to be going somewhere and, therefore, it must have a guide. Others feel a sense of moral "oughtness" which they believe has been placed in them by some great universal being. Some feel creation is filled with cause-and-effect relationships; therefore, there must have been a First Cause. Still others simply have an emotional feeling that there must be something greater than themselves. We need not dwell on these arguments here because our concern is with the very different, biblical God.

Before there was any clear-cut awareness of God as Creator or Redeemer as we understand it, there was a call from out of the blue,

41

literally, and one heroic man responded. With such a man God made a covenant which did as much to define the man as it did the God who made him. It defines all who have the same faith.

The philosopher has said glibly, "Know thyself," as if it were all that easy. Long before Freud made us aware of the war between our glands and our upbringing, the apostle Paul cried out for deliverance from the battle that raged in his mind and his heart, doing the things he didn't want to do and not doing the things he wanted to do (see Romans 7:15). Why are we so contrary, and how will we possibly know ourselves when this kind of confusion prevails? Long before Paul, God was giving us the Answer.

Thus, our early awareness of God grew out of the commitment of a man. We grant that God took the initiative. We believe that our God is a God who acts. Otherwise, our faith is merely our own human manipulation. But as God acted in history, a very human, down-to-earth person responded: a tough, strong, honest person who was not about to give in easily, not about to give his allegiance to gods he could possibly doubt. If he could have believed in other gods, he would have.

It must not be lost on us that our faith in God has an essentially historic nature. It was a call to a man in a given country in human history. All the speculation and all of the bull sessions ultimately have to come back to this historic action on the part of God, a voice that was heard by a heroic, tough, honest person.

Christian people should never allow themselves to be involved in idle, philosophical speculation about First Causes or Unmoved Movers or Moral Imperatives. We must recognize that when we exhaust all of these arguments and turn everywhere we please, we come back to the irreducible call to covenant and commitment, the radical call which Abraham first heard. This is how our God is defined, and, interestingly enough, it's how Abraham was defined. If Jesus is the Clue to God's purpose, God the Father is the clue to our purpose as human beings. We are called to covenant, to relationship, to a plan and a purpose. For Abraham it was to bless all the nations of the earth through his offspring who would be as sands on the seashore. This same Abraham is called the father of our own faith in the same God. We, too, are called by this jealous God who will have no other god before him—all of our other "faiths" are overwhelmed by the last and greatest "call," the call of God to us to be his people called for his purpose.

5

The Joy of Job

We saw in chapter 4 how radical honesty was called forth in Abraham and how Abraham was shaped by his openness to God. Job is another person in the Old Testament who through his response to God shows us something more about this God who really never can be known completely. We learn more about the biblical God, as we said, from looking at those who people the Old Testament than we can learn from philosophers. The God of the Old Testament is a God who acts on persons, who forms a People and is thereby known by his People. These various persons, in different circumstances, all hold to one central truth—that the Lord God of Israel is one God and there is none other besides him.

It may seem incongruous to call Job joyous. But Job is maligned by the common gossip which often passes for biblical interpretation. Job has been popularly held up as the epitome of patience, and perhaps of passive stupidity, for putting up with God's meanness. In truth Job was anything but patient. He knew too much about God and took him too seriously to stand by passively when all those terrible things were poured out on him in spite of his righteous relationship and faithfulness to God. Job had been shaped by his joy in his wonderful Lord, and his long ordeal ended with a shout of affirmation even though no explanation is ever given for God's abuse of Job.

Job was not content to listen to the glib little explanations, no matter how well intended, of his "friends" and comforters. His God could not be so easily explained. Deep joy had been his prior experience, and nothing could change that. No experience and no excuse could move him from his confidence in a good God. Granted, Job ranted and railed, but that was out of his honesty and confidence. A person insecure or uncertain about God would not feel free to rant and rave. We see this over and over again with the prophets who have such a close and confident relationship to God that they feel free to shake their fists, complain, and protest. These are the marks of integrity, of feeling, and of relationship. There was nothing phony, nothing of sweetness and light, nothing superficial or mawkishly sentimental about them. Their pain was real and their God was real.

Job had taken the same plunge as Abraham, and there was no turning back. If God wanted to punish him, even though he could not see the reason or any justification for it, then so be it. He said with many others down through the ages, "Though he send me to Hell, yet will I trust him" (see Job 13:15, KJV). God is just that powerful (sovereign) and requires that kind of commitment and allegiance from all of us.

"The Problem of Evil"

Philosophers call this kind of ordeal "the problem of evil." We do not need to be philosophers to know how wicked and stupid the world is. All we need do if death and grief have not already touched us personally is to read the daily headlines: children dead of fire or cancer, divorce, greed, and seemingly natural disasters which leave only heartbreak in their wake. How can we possibly believe in a God who either causes or allows this to happen? Either God is good and impotent to stop evil, or he allows evil and is therefore not good. He is either good and powerless or powerful and evil.

It becomes obvious to all of us that the wicked of this world prosper and that there is no assurance for those who believe God that they will get a better deal than those who do not trust God. If believing in God is not a good deal, why bother? If there is no reward for faith, why should we have any traffic at all with God? It makes as much sense to go on without faith as it does to trust such a God. This is good reasoning if making sense and good reasoning are the point. But faith in the God of Abraham and Job does not make sense in the usual sense. One of the primary theological truths which we can learn best from the Old Testament is that God is a God who shows himself but does not always explain himself. It could even be said that he never completely explains himself. We are changed and shaped, therefore, by revelation and response and not by reason. This seems terribly unjust. Certainly it must have seemed so to Job. It will never seem otherwise. There is simply no explanation for why the wicked prosper or why evil exists in the world. It is just there. Philosophers do their best to explain, some holding to one theory and some to another. Some say God would if he could but he can't. Some say he could if he would but he won't. Each camp has some reason for either God's impotence or his coldness, but no reason is satisfying. The joy of the Lord is the joy which comes beyond all consideration of pleasure and pain. God is the origin of all. He is the end of all. If you settle for little bargains of your own liking, then you are bargaining with a little God of your own making.

God's Sovereignty and Power

In the Book of Job, it is not just idle poetry that Satan had to go to God for permission when he wanted to plague and bug Job. God is all-sovereign and all-powerful, and the Bible makes it very clear, though not philosophically acceptable, that God is the Creator of all which we can possibly know. If this makes him the author of evil, then we need to accept that (as Isaiah seems to in Isaiah 45:7). It is better to believe that God is sovereign and Lord over everything than to have Satan, evil, or our puny human understanding hold the same importance or power as God. God must be greater than any evil or any human experience.

Job's joy was not rooted in a God who could be manipulated or explained. God just was and he was just God. This creates in the faithful a joyous faith that cannot be touched or thwarted by life's experience. It is this certainty which Jesus referred to when he said the world could indeed kill our bodies (see Matthew 10:28) but our joy was secure in the God who (as Paul insisted in Romans 8:35) was beyond, over, under, and in front of death, who has dominion over it.

We are thus shaped by our faith in such a God; "we are what we believe."

Job was not patient. He was very human. He suffered and he railed against God. But nowhere in his railing, in his discomfort, in his loneliness, or in his suffering was there any suggestion that God was puny, despicable, or intimidated by human demands for understanding. Job praises God in the end because that's all he can do. And yet that is everything. To alter this kind of trust, this kind of profound joy, is to alter the essential message of the Old Testament which is that God is the great Shaper, Humanizer, the One who makes us into something different from what we possibly could be without him. In the process he shows us something of himself, even as he shows us ourselves.

45

6

Moses, the Medium

We have been taught rather mindlessly that compromise is evil. But God compromises again and again through history in order that mere mortal eyes can stand the glory of his awful (full of awe) gaze. Such was the case with Moses, another in whom we can see God showing himself as he shapes persons.

This definition of compromise may seen inconsistent with what we said earlier about the radical response of Abraham or the blind trust of Job. Perhaps it is, but foolish consistency, as Emerson suggests, "is the hobgoblin of little minds."[1] Compromise is a facet of God which we can't neglect in any theological consideration.

God's Compromise in Moses

Moses was such a compromise. We have read of Abraham and ancient history. We will marvel at the intimacy of the prophets who had a personal relationship with the high and holy God, who formed and fashioned the Jews into a people with a moral conscience. But we must not neglect that giant in the Old Testament: Moses. He was reluctant to respond; he had physical handicaps; he was not a great preacher; he had murder on his record. In a society such as ours, dependent on credentials, where one mistake is carried forward in our computerized pedigree, we ought to be able to understand what a great compromise Moses was. It must not be lost on us that this compromised person, who caused God to compromise himself by

[1] Ralph Waldo Emerson, *Self-Reliance* (Mount Vernon, N.Y.: Peter Pauper Press, 1979), p. 21.

using such a person, was the father of the Law. To see Law as a compromise at the outset will help us to understand the struggles of the apostle Paul in laying the Law to rest. The Law was extremely important in God's revelation to his people and exceedingly important in our understanding of ourselves.

God gave to Moses the requirements and the rules to "hold over" the people of Israel, a bridge between the great patriarchs and the gospel, between Abraham and Jesus.

Moses himself is an interesting combination, a passionate prophet and a cool lawyer. You'll remember he had a fierce temper which resulted in a murder in his youth and later in frightful rages against the disobedient people who in their impatience had talked his brother, Aaron, into making an idol, the infamous golden calf. But God nevertheless prevailed in his pursuit of the man Moses. When necessary, God even provided a duplicate copy of the rules he had given Moses to guide the people of Israel toward their destination as the holy people of God, who were to carry the blessing to all the world, even as God had called Abraham for that purpose.

Moses was to lead the people from servitude to freedom. The Exodus is not only something ancient but is also a condition which applies to every generation, to human beings in bondage and servitude unable to fulfill their destiny. It is out of that servitude and evil that God calls, and not only calls but leads, and not only leads but provides daily bread (manna) to his people. The Exodus is the symbol of human sinfulness and deliverance. But what's worse, as the ancient people preferred to live in servitude rather than in the wilderness with God, trusting God for their daily bread, so we prefer sin to salvation, darkness to light. So it has always been, and so it shall always be until we are fully and finally saved—God revealing himself as the true God, in whom we must put our trust, being forced to compromise himself again and again by reaching down to us in our passionate temper (as in the case of Moses) and in our servitude (as in the case of the people of Israel).

The Law, Another of God's Compromises

A people under the Law were different from a people under the prophets or a nomadic people with stories told by campfire to hold them together. Such storytelling from generation to generation is called oral tradition; we in our day would call it folk singing. Even when the people of God insisted on a king, a king "like other pagan nations had" (see 1 Samuel 8:5-6), they still needed the Law to distinguish them from other peoples.

We must recognize that Moses and the Law were a mixed blessing. Compromises are always mixed. God chose Moses for the next step in the development of his people. Beyond their wandering as nomads, the Law not only told them how to behave religiously, but it also showed them a reflection of creation. It helped them to live lives which would abide by "nature," God's nature, God's creation. They could see themselves as law-abiding, or "nature-abiding," and this was good, meaningful, and helpful.

Obviously, the acceptance of the Law by the people was not the first time that they considered the matter of sin. The remarkable accounts in the creation stories in the first three chapters of Genesis deal with the root and source of sin, or estrangement of Creator and creation. But the Law was an attempt to be right in the eyes of a just God, a means of being objective, of setting up norms which would coincide with God's creation, adherence to which would mean that the people were righteous.

It is worth noting here, even as we consider this giant, Moses, that it would not be long in the history of God's people before the Law would become inadequate and something more would have to be breathed into the people. That something more was the prophets. In some ways we could say "restored" rather than "breathed into" because the prophets had been a powerful influence in the lives of the people of God before the Law became codified and acceptable. But even the prophets and the Law together would need an infusion of God's own Spirit. But before we get to the discussion of God's full Spirit, we ought to take a look at the third category of material in the Old Testament—in addition to the Law and the Prophets—that body of material called the Writings.

Thus, so far we see that God always adapts himself even though he remains the sovereign and righteous God. He compromises, coming in forms that give us clues, even as he came finally in the perfect Clue. All through the Old Testament we see God working through prophet and through Law as well as through poem and song to gain a response from his people. He didn't turn away because his own perfection was offended by sin, but, rather, he persisted in calling the people back again and again from their spiritual adultery and idolatry. The Law is one of those grand compromises of God, and Moses was the Medium.

7

Poem Power

There are some things we can only sing about. Words without ecstatic chants are inadequate to express some human experiences. We recognize that many things in life need careful, legal, and scientific explanations. Thus, there is no end to the making of books. Our law libraries and our research centers welcome microfilm technology as a blessing. But there are other human experiences so difficult to crystallize that words can only allude to the meaning. For these things we need poems and songs. To put it another way, when God comes to us in these profound experiences, only songs and hymns can adequately shape us, to say nothing about giving proper praise to God. We shout praises when our minds are literally beside themselves with a faith so certain that it cannot be contained in words. As a child begins to skip and dance when built-up energy and enthusiasm reach the point where walking will simply not serve, so human beings burst into songs. In the Old Testament an important place is held by the Psalms, sometimes called the Hymnbook of the Second Temple.

The Psalms, a Reflection of Our Theology of Creation

The Psalms are different from any other material in the Bible. They are included in that group of Old Testament books called Writings. Not only did the ancient people of God distill these songs for use in their temple worship, but the songs also continued to be the source of deep comfort and joy in all generations, even now, precisely at those times when arguments and easy explanations are beside the point. The Twenty-third Psalm, for instance, which is "said" at gravesides and sick beds, speaks far beyond the mere words.

It is no accident that a good deal of what we think about the unprovable parts of life in this world are contained in these psalms. Our theology of creation, except for the first three chapters of Genesis, which are themselves most poetic, is reflected in the Psalms. The creation as the workmanship of Almighty God the Creator is beyond any scientific treatise or proof. We are both pathetic and embarrassing, if not bordering on blasphemy, when we attempt to force the beauty and power of the creation Psalms or the creation accounts in Genesis into the little boxes to which science must by definition confine itself. Science measures. Psalms praise. There are no careful measurements in the first three chapters of Genesis or in these hymns which speak of God's prowess and power over nature and over creation. To try to make a scientific textbook out of a song, to make a technical geological journal out of Genesis is to settle for far less than these powerful poems have to offer.

Scholars teach us that the creation materials in Genesis were added to the literature of the people of God at a late date and that the Psalms were actually earlier than the Genesis accounts. Some Christians are upset by this, but it would seem to me to be exciting that the longer this people lived with God, the more they became certain of him as Creator and thus could write the lasting and beautiful, infallible if you please, account of his relationship to us and to the world, after having been themselves shaped by the living God.

If we think about it, the beginnings of Genesis really don't tell us as much about creation in general as they do about our relationship to it. Again, this is exciting rather than distressing. We learn about ourselves when we read the Psalms; we learn that we are in the image of God.

Made in God's Image

Without question, in the Bible all creation is attributed to God. There is no room for debate. It's a matter of faith, but it must not escape us that we are dynamically defined as persons by that faith. We are in God's image. That insight defines us more than it does God, though it does obviously also tell us something about will and the power of choice, about the ability to take certain courses of action, about not being ruled by instinct; it tells us something about learning from our experiences and building on them (we call this education) and something about new beginnings; all these mark us humans off from all the rest of God's creation.

In some mysterious way something of God himself is in us. God speaks with us in the garden, and all is well. We hear God say we are left in charge of his creation; we are to name the animals and to be stewards over them. To name anything is to know that thing, to assume Godlike power over it, to separate, to catalog. To command and to change is to assume something of the very creative and sovereign powers of God. These are not scientific declarations as much as they are profound insights into relationships between God, his creation, and persons in his image.

What a difference it makes to our view of ourselves and others to believe that we are not animals or collections of protein which by some chance are able to look at themselves and think about themselves! What a difference it makes in our politics and the way we spend our lives and our resources! These are great value judgments which are to be sung about rather than to be debated. God created us male and female that we might know each other, that we might experience communion and community. We never feel so good as when we make someone else feel good or when someone else loves us. So it was in Eden: perfect fellowship.

The Fall

But life is not always like that; it's obvious to the most primitive that loving and sharing is not as "natural" as we might like, at least not after the fall described in Genesis 3. Whatever else that means, it also means that something happened to make that which was natural unnatural, something which could be redeemed only by the supernatural.

So the songwriters of old, struggling with their own understanding of themselves and the rugged world of storms and enemies, tell us of a "fall." Dissatisfied with looking to God for everything, Adam (man) had to try for it all, the whole "apple" as it were. God could not be God and allow that to happen. So Eden ended; man and woman would "do their thing," work or birthing as the case may be, in pain and sweat. The ancient people of God who wrote and thought about these things interpreted everything over against a jealous God who was very unlike the gods of their neighbors, gods who could be manipulated by fertility rites and by all sorts of appeasement. Those gods were made of wood and stone and were simply puppets of the people who made them. Those neighbors with their gods (baalim) had the same need to know, the same human experiences, as did the Jews, but the answer of the Jew was radical and different. The Jew insisted that there was only one God who would brook no competition. If life was ugly and uncertain, it had to be interpreted nevertheless over against that one God.

There was none other, none greater. We often take this radical idea for granted because we have heard the First Commandment so many times it has lost its impact and thrust.

So we have the Hebrew Psalms, the instruments of regular worship whereby relationships could be affirmed and restored. Many parts of the book of Psalms are clearly intended for liturgical use, that is, in worship services. The ordinary worshipers would respond even as we do today sometimes. Other psalms belong in neither of these categories but seem to be related to private devotion.

In any event, we place these hymns and songs and expressions of poetry alongside the books of Leviticus, Exodus, and Deuteronomy, and the Ten Commandments.

The people of God had a deep and profound reverence for the very name of God. The prophets would preach and rail, and the Law would be laid down; but all was to no avail unless there was singing, unless there was worship, and unless there was reverence.

God thereby shapes us into reverent human beings; he is the humanizer and shows us that we shall never be human unless we are also worshiping the One who is our Creator and has made us in his image. We learn about ourselves as much as we learn about God.

8

A Prophet-Making Business

We've seen honest commitment, even in the face of great suffering, when we've looked at Abraham and Job. Now we need to think about a great part of the Old Testament known as the Prophets.

There's a great deal of confusion in contemporary times about this word "prophet," or about "prophecy." There was even some confusion back in the Old Testament days. Distinctions were made between true and false prophets. Prophecy itself went through a development in which it moved from mere and erratic ecstasy to a consistent experience in the lives of some of the greatest of the Old Testament characters. The key word here is experience, back to which we will come in just a minute.

In modern times we often equate prophecy with fortune-telling. The so-called modern prophet uses texts from the Old Testament and from Revelation in the New Testament the way a fortune-teller uses leaves in the bottom of a tea cup. But such prophecy is not biblical. Prophecy does not have to do primarily with fortune-telling; it is not foretelling as much as forthtelling.

In fact, it would be fair to say that in the Old Testament very little distinction was made between past, present, and future. When the prophet had a message, he preached it with all the certainty of God. God was neither past, present, nor future, but always in the present tense: "I Am" was the way God described himself to his people. The prophets just accepted that and were not concerned with telling the future except to show that the unfolding of history would be the sign of God's power over time, place, and nation; past, present, and future; and all geographical locations. Except as the details of the prophecy made the message more graphic and real, there was no inordinate concern with calendars, with charts predicting the end of the world, or details about the conquest of God's people for their sin. The Old Testament prophet is in marked contrast to the contemporary prophet who often ignores history even though he seems to be talking about it and speaks to a cultic group rather than to the whole people of God. Let's sort out some of the characteristics of those ancient prophets.

Characteristics of the Ancient Prophets

If there was one thing of which the prophet was certain, it was that God speaks; and when he speaks, his people are able to hear him. Without question, God is high and lifted up, beyond our human understanding. In the Old Testament people believed this fact even more than we do. They had a reverence for the awe-full Almighty which the modern secular mind cannot experience. They had a reverence which has been lost on us because we are products of a so-called literate society which has locked arms with reason and scientific proof to the point where we have lost much of our sense of wonder. This is unfortunate, but about all we can do about it is to realize that something indeed has gone out of us. So when we say that the prophets believed God could speak to his people and that his people could hear, we are not saying anything light or easy to grasp. It was a shock to their systems, to the very nature of a people, politically as well as theologically God's people. To believe that God, who acts on their behalf and who called them in Abraham, also would speak to them, especially when they were out of line, was important and most impressive.

Though there are some beautiful, positive teachings in the Prophets, basically what is there is negative. This has disturbed some Christians who equate a sunny disposition with the depths of redemption. But as one scholar, in the face of objection to such pessimism, put it, ". . . moral pessimism is preferable to immoral optimism."[1]

The prophets were raised up because Israel, in the plain biblical phrase, had gone whoring after other gods. They were unfaithful. Hosea was to use his own broken marriage as an example of how Israel had run off, even as his own wife had left him and gone down the block to live with her lover.

[1] H. Wheeler Robinson, *The Religious Ideas of the Old Testament* (London: Gerald Duckworth & Co., Ltd., 1952), p. 121.

But it does not take a great deal of insight to understand along with Jeremiah that if God would build anew, he must first clear the ground. We can see in this pessimism of the prophets a silver lining. God, high and lifted up, most holy and awe-full, must love his people a great deal if he would break forth in prophets with a certain and sure message for his people. The prophets literally became the "mouth of God" to his people, a sign of love and affection even though the message was one of wrath and condemnation. Those whom God loves he also chastises. The prophets show us a living, acting, interested God, interested in the details of history, the fortunes of his people, and, above all, the way they responded to their fortunes. When they failed to give Almighty God the credit, there was a prophet to challenge and confront them. The prophets were concerned to reflect God's own morality in the face of his people's immorality.

This raises obvious questions with us. Do we believe that God still speaks so that his people can understand, or do we feel that God has "abandoned" us, as some say? Is it possible that God speaks only to some in our day even as he spoke only to the ancient prophets? Could our experience today be pretty much the same as Israel's when the immediate experience of God to a few was a warming fire for the rest of the people?

A second characteristic of the prophets, whether we are thinking of the earlier ones, such as Amos, or the later ones, such as some of the minor prophets or whom scholars call "Second Isaiah" (Isaiah 40-66), is that the prophets were individuals, highly personal with all sorts of weird and strange idiosyncrasies. Many scholars feel that they had what we today would call mental illness of one sort or another. Since we know so little about mental illness even today, all of our scientific research notwithstanding, I doubt if it is profitable for us to diagnose the prophets with contemporary psychiatric terminology. There is no reason why God shouldn't use someone who is strange to bring his word anymore than it is for him to use someone strange to do a brilliant piece of work in our day. We refer to the first as a looney and the second as a genius. But God is God over all of us including those of us who might have physiological problems, mental problems, or simply see life differently from the rest. It "ill-behooves" us to categorize people and dismiss them as being outside of God's providence simply because they are different. If anything is true, it is that the prophets were different, highly individual, and definitely not in the social register. They were not on anybody's favorite party list. They were not establishment.

In the history of Israel the Law, the temple, and the priests played the major part in the continuity of the Covenant first made with Abraham (and, in a sense, with Noah and Adam before that) and then with those who came later. God's authority was placed with the priest, the law, and the regular worship in the temple. It has always been thus. It is still true that the institution we call the church, with whatever authority we establish there in the leadership and/or in the sacrament (ordinances), is the stabilizing continuity. But continuity through ritual is capable of subtle corruption if not blatant deviance. Therefore, personal and ecstatic individuals filled with God's immediacy need to be raised up to challenge the prosaic stability of the Law and the temple, the lack of spirit in the traditional institutions of worship.

The Hebrew word for prophet may mean "bubble out"; most of the prophets acted like they had something within them that was just going to boil and bubble like a fire in their bones, as Jeremiah put it, until it got out (see Jeremiah 20:9). They were literally people possessed, personally and individually.

We must not in our modern times forget this prophetic necessity through all of Israel's history. We tend, as they did in that day, to look at anyone whose message is "different," unduly pessimistic, and unusually abrasive to our present set of values as one who is to be dismissed or constrained. "Managed" is the dreadful word which modern medicine uses in reference to such people.

There is no question that some ecstasy is simply an aberration or, for want of a better word, mental illness. It was true back in the days of the Old Testament as well, and the false prophets needed to be sorted out from the true. But we must nevertheless always be sensitive to the need for the prophet and to recognize persons who have a highly individualized concept of their faith. They should not be dismissed out of hand but should be listened to with at least some sensitivity toward grasping their message.

In this regard it should be noted that the prophets came from outside the church, as it were. There is no exact equation between the church of their day and the church in our day, but for the most part the prophets were not establishment insiders. They were people from outside, laity if you please, from all walks of life. From Amos, a farmworker, to Isaiah, an educated and cultivated patrician. But without exception they all, even the later ones who were concerned about rebuilding the temple and the priestly religion, were highly individual people who believed that God's ability to speak to his people was going to be through them and they would not be shut up.

58

Jeremiah prophesied for forty-five years, three years of which he went around the street with his yoke, predicting the disaster that was to come to the people of God because of their unfaithfulness.

A third characteristic of the prophets is the pessimism and abrasiveness to which I've already alluded. The prophets were in the main invariably negative. They represented a personal attempt by a personal God to bring a people, not just an abstract nation, back to himself. The people had drifted and wandered and gone after false gods. They were insensitive to the poor; they were bloated and glutted with luxury; they had turned in upon themselves for their worship and had made little idols which told them, as we might expect, just what they wanted to hear. They were not being faithful to the Covenant, to the promise which God had made through Abraham not only to them but also to the whole world. Our destiny today is dependent upon those people, and they were not fulfilling their obligation or their promise. God, therefore, needed to clash with them. The prophetic ministry could be described as God's clash with the world, with his people who were to be the core of redemption for the world.

Religion, especially contemporary religion, ofttimes degenerates into positive thinking about ourselves and the world in which we live. There's much to be said for "possibility thinking" and for an emphasis upon the living grace and power of God. There is no question that God wants good for his world, that he looked upon creation and saw that it was good, and that it shall be good again. He will accomplish his redemption, and we don't want to become so negative that we don't understand the primary thrust of God's message: positive healing, restructuring, and reconciling. But if we believe in those things without understanding the nature of our self-deception, the nature of our sin which says to us that we are good when really we are bad, we are going to be of all persons most deluded. This was the condition of those ancient people. God was just as positive, just as loving, and just as gracious then as he is now. Nevertheless, prophets were needed then as they're needed now to remind human beings that the values which they hold and that the things they think are so cute and good are ofttimes an abomination in God's sight. It is the very nature of our sin that we will get fat and sloppy and be unaware of the radical nature of God's redemption. To take the negative view, because of the radical nature of our sin and its penetration of our entire personality, is to become "untrustworthy" judges of what is good and bad. God raises up people to confront us, to clash with us, to place in our way a living word which stops us and makes us think

59

about just what God wants from us and just what it is we are doing, or not doing, to fulfill God's demands and God's promise.

We want our church services quiet; we speak in hushed tones. We want the music soft and sweet. If it must be loud, then please, we insist, confine it to Easter morning. For the most part we don't want raucous ecstacies but prefer quiet meditations and hushed tones, darkness with the only light to disturb our strained optic nerves filtered through beautiful stained-glass windows.

Such was the condition of the people in the days of the prophets and, for that matter, all through Israel's history. God could not tolerate such delusion, such comfort bought at the expense of the poor, the impoverished. He sent prophets to rub the people the wrong way, to wake them up, to make them understand that they were not dealing with a God who was their bellhop, their pet, but the holy God who had made them, a jealous God who insisted that he be first in everything.

In our own day we need to be aware that our worship cannot always be hushed and quiet, that our understanding of God cannot be separated from the harsh headlines of the daily newspaper or the voice of doom which comes from the anchorman on the six o'clock news.

And that brings us to still another characteristic of the prophet: that the prophet was practical. The prophets did not participate in vague or abstract ranting and raving. Their preaching was particular. It had to do with what we've come to call social action. There was nothing of "pie in the sky" and the "sweet by and by" in their preaching. It had to do with the people to whom they were speaking, and they pointed their fingers, even as Nathan did at David. True prophets were separated from the false prophets not by whether or not they could tell fortunes but by whether or not their sense of history, of day-to-day events, could be convincingly understood by people who listened to them. Prophets never talked to themselves, nor were they ever sweet, pious little things who could be dismissed as "Sunday school types." They were rough, tough characters who came right out of the community, preaching to those around them in the cities and the streets.

As we've seen, the prophets had a sense of the eternal God who spoke through them, even though many of them were extremely reluctant to carry his message, as was Jeremiah. The people needed to listen at the peril of their very existence. The prophets were, to use an overworked word in our contemporary parlance, "relevant," with a vengeance.

The Message of the Prophets to Us Today

When we separate, as we often do in modern times, social action and individual salvation, we are making a division that is not biblical. Certainly in the Old Testament these highly individualistic people we call prophets, certain of their experience with God and the personal immediacy of their message, also related that message at every point to social action: to widows and orphans, the hungry, the oppressed, and even, as we would think of it, to the Department of Defense, and offense, for that matter.

Thus, we need in every age to be shaped by prophetic consciousness. We need to make prophets that are not to be confused with profits. Preachers are needed in our day who are not a part of the church or any other establishment, who do not draw their salaries from the people to whom they speak. Show me a prophet who needs to make a profit, and I'll show you a polite prophet. The prophetic stream throughout the Old Testament was anything but polite, anything but time-serving, anything but afraid. They may have been pessimistic, unhappy, and perhaps even crazy. But God raised them up, spoke through them, and used their eccentricities to his glory. He shaped his people by the prophetic consciousness. It was necessary then, and it is necessary now. We need to understand ourselves as people who will become fat and lazy and go to sleep. Both from within and without ourselves there needs to be that prophetic voice not only to remind us of our evil propensities but also to make us understand that God speaks immediately and directly to us as well.

PART III

The Holy Spirit: Lover

9

The Church Social

Around the church we use the word "fellowship" rather loosely. We think in terms of a picnic, a church supper, or a small group going out to eat together after church or just to enjoy one another's company. There's nothing wrong with this use of the word "fellowship"; in fact, it is profoundly right.

The Profoundest Meaning of Church Fellowship

But the church social has the profoundest of meanings. It means that we cannot be Christian alone. It means that to be shaped by God, in addition to all that we've seen from our thinking in earlier chapters on creation and the Old Testament, all that we've understood about Christ as the clue to creation, is to be a body. We are the arm or the leg or the eye, as the apostle Paul puts it in one of his letters to a local church (1 Corinthians 12). None of us can be complete without the other; whether we be an unattractive part of the body or an attractive part, each is important and none is to be denigrated. The church is corporate; it is social; it involves many. The church is always a church social.

Social means relationship. And relationship means more than one connected in some way. There are all sorts of connections and myriad kinds of relationships in the world. Most of the worldly relationships, if not all, are based on merit. Someone passes muster and is accepted by another. A relationship ensues, and whatever it was that the one person liked becomes the basis of the relationship, of the fellowship, if you please. The relationship is based on having something, anything, in common. But just anything is not always sufficient for relationships; and if a given relationship suddenly finds itself having changed, with little any longer in common, it dissolves. Witness the divorce rate, in light of marriage supposedly being one of the more serious relationships in our society. It is easily, too easily, dissolved because the two persons no longer have anything in common. Suddenly there is no basis for the relationship.

Thus, the more a relationship has in common and the more persistent that common value is, the stronger the relationship. If a relationship were to be built on the strongest common element in the world (and out of it); if that common thing were eternal and forever; if that common thing were the totally free gift of another, a gift totally beyond earning; then that relationship would be a profound one indeed. The fellowship in such a relationship would be markedly different from any about which this world knows.

The church is just such a fellowship. The church is a "social," created by its Lord and God as founder and giver of himself. What the members of the church have in common is this relationship with God—not something which they find attractive in one another; not something laid on by the world; not credentials, money, education, or good looks—none of these. The gift is the living love of God in Jesus Christ for all persons. Thus, the fellowship generated is "human-kind-wide," worldwide. Nothing generates a deeper fellowship than such a great gift, such an irresistible gift, a gift beyond human manipulation.

When that gift is given and received, it makes love; it is the great love maker.

The Holy Spirit, Instigator of Fellowship

Traditionally and rather mindlessly, I dare say, we have thought of the Holy Spirit as the inspirer of the individual. But we must think more profoundly of the Holy Spirit as the enabler of love, as the instigator of community, of fellowship, of a true "social."

Paul ends one of his letters to the church at Corinth: "Greet one another with a holy kiss, live in peace, grace, and love, and the *fellowship of the Holy Spirit* be with you" (see 2 Corinthians 13:11-14). The Holy Spirit is the creator of fellowship. The Holy Spirit generates love one for the other. Greet one another with a holy kiss; live in peace, grace, and love.

It's one thing to define love. That's done every day in countless ways, sometimes well, sometimes only adding to the confusion. Certainly love is a word basic to our experience, and yet it's one which is so universal in its currency that it easily loses its meaning. But having said that, our problem really isn't in defining love as much as finding the power which will allow us to form fellowship and to be with one another in grace and peace.

How easily we fall out with one another, even in the church! We're so quickly unfaithful to one another. So easily frightened, fearful and closed, keeping our affection within rigid confines, undeveloped and shriveled, and leaving and separating from one another at the slightest provocation.

"How do I love thee? Let me count the ways," says the familiar poem of Browning. That's a tender, romantic poem, but the question needs to be put in much more practical and theological terms. The question becomes not so much, "How do I love thee? Let me count the ways," but, "How *can* I love thee? How can I find the way?"

Because you're different from me, you hold a different view, you wear different clothing, or your hair is long, your skin is a different color, or you hum and sing all the time, or you worry about the right things at the wrong time or the wrong things at the right time, or because you're too attractive for me seriously to consider responsible intimacy—for all these reasons we are closed. Our real problem becomes not so much, "Let me organize and think about the ways I love you," but, rather, "Where will I find the power? Who shall deliver me from the prison houses of anxiety? Who will make me a lover?" The answer simply is God, who by his Spirit is himself the great Lover, the Creator of community, intimacy, peace, and grace.

The Biblical Description of Fellowship

We need to think seriously about the figures of speech we find throughout Scripture which refer to fellowship and community. The chief one in the New Testament is marriage. The church is the bride of Jesus Christ; the church people are obviously married to one another and to Christ. He is the bridegroom and we are the bride. The very essence of heaven will be perfect community, intimacy, and fellowship—in effect, a perfect marriage with one another and with God. Another word for it is fellowship. The power and the enabling for such warming intimacy come from God.

It's God's Holy Spirit which creates this marriage, which maintains this community and relationship. There is no discussion of community in the New Testament whatsoever without mention of the Holy Spirit of God.

We've been too influenced, especially as Baptists, by philosopher John Locke and his social contract theory of government. This theory clearly influenced our American Constitution, but we cannot allow it to influence overly our thinking about the church. We must understand God as the Father, as the Son, but also as the Spirit, as lover. We Protestants in the United States have seen ourselves all too often strictly in terms of voluntarism. We've assumed we have no obligation to one another unless we volunteer to have that association, unless we suit one another. We assume no commitment to one another unless we find one another compatible and attractive. When we don't like what we see or feel, we, as rugged individualists, withdraw.

We put a great stress on conscience, and so we should, but the conscience is never all that private. It is, I agree, the essence of our selves. But our selves develop only in marriage, community, and commitment to one another, only in society. The "church social" means not only going out to dinner together but also living together in peace and grace, educating and instructing one another. We'll deal further with this later when we deal with authority.

It is interesting that no worldly organization is ever built without regard for merit. Sooner or later somebody sits in judgment and says you can come in or you must stay out. Unfortunately the church too often tries to emulate that society, making goodness or some other merit a criterion for admittance. But God loved us while we were yet sinners. The initiative, as we saw with Abraham, is always his. His Holy Spirit moves out to us creating a love which was not there before. Love which we feel for one another is not dependent upon what we think about one another, whether or not we pass muster with one another, but, rather, upon God's work in Abraham and Isaac and Jacob, Moses, the prophets, Jesus Christ, and now, following Pentecost (the birthday of the church), in us.

Discrimination takes on new meaning for Christians. Instead of discriminating against those who are unlike ourselves, those who represent unpopular views or unpopular cultures, we now discriminate only on the possibility that persons will receive the message that God is personal, that he loves them, that he loves us all, and that he makes us into a "social," into human beings who belong together. He shapes us by the gift of his Spirit and gives us the power to love that which is by all worldly logic unattractive.

Sometimes it's hard to know which is worse, adultery or adultery in reverse. In ordinary definitions of adultery there is betrayal of trust and the degeneration of commitment one to another. But the opposite of adultery is even worse. A shriveled withdrawal from the risk of relationships, the very relationships God is seeking to establish, is also a betrayal. We may not be betraying persons, but we're betraying God. His Holy Spirit is lover and he can no more be betrayed in the design of his love for all of us than we can betray a wife or husband, or friend for that matter.

Paul talks of the holy kiss. Kisses as we think of them discriminate, and yet the holy kiss is indiscriminate. It is not as we often think of kisses in general—as intimacies to be guarded carefully. Rather, it's a gesture generated in us by the love of God and given to one another without regard for the natural propensities to beauty or attractiveness common to our "natural" feelings. This kiss is a discriminate intimacy made indiscriminate by the largeness of God's heart and the breadth and profundity of his love.

When we talk about getting together, we usually mean with those with whom we agree. If it's with those with whom we disagree, we have all kinds of ways of manipulating, hoping that if they'll just do a little more of their homework, they will come around to agreeing with us. If they will just shape up a little bit, they will be acceptable. But God's power and Spirit comes to us and turns all of our lives into a great and grand church social whether we are ready or not, whether we like it or not, whether we agree with one another or not.

God's Spirit and heart is larger than any division.

You can see the scandal that is created in the world when we are so dense and so insensitive to Jesus' prayers for us—for instance, as he talks about our being one in the Father (see John 17) with him and by the power of the Holy Spirit.

Ecumenism, or one church, is not an option. It is the very nature of God's body. When we are separated as we are into 252 Protestant denominations, to say nothing about our cleavage with our Christian brethren in the Roman and Greek churches, we should be much in prayer and deeply concerned if we do not feel intimately in fellowship. We are being shaped, but it cannot be by the Spirit of God if we do not increasingly see ourselves as lovers, in love with one another and in love with God.

It is hard for us to understand what it is we're missing when we think of the church of God as just our little church on the corner or our little group. Some of us struggle in small churches and small communities. Our behavior and conduct is not particularly sociable as far as the rest of the world or perhaps even the community is concerned. The story is told of a skeptic who was passing the door of a small country church one Sunday morning following the service. The church was small and struggling, and as the minister stood at the door greeting the few people coming out, the skeptic called out to the pastor, "Not many in church this morning, eh, Reverend?" The minister said, "Not at all, my son. There are thousands and tens of thousands here this morning." That minister was a theologian with a profound understanding of God, of his Holy Spirit as lover, and of the church as one body in this place and in all time and eternity. The communion of the saints is invisible as well as visible.

If we are to be shaped by God, it will be as we understand that we have been turned into one gigantic church social with all Christians of all ages and in every clime.

10

No Other Name

Having known the Great Lover, one of the things that bothers loving people are those Scripture references which insist there is no other name by which we can be saved (see Acts 4:12) or that "no man cometh unto the Father, but by me" (see John 14:6), the very words of Jesus. There are millions and millions who have lived and died without ever having had the chance to hear about Jesus. No matter how sterling our missionary effort in the past, there remain great nations of the world where the percentage of Christians is exceedingly small. Those who are dead and gone have no chance. And even of those who are alive, millions will never hear. And then, of course, there are those who have heard and have preferred their own religious experience and faith: Buddhists, Muslims, animists of various kinds, spiritualists, and we must not forget in our own nation millions of secularists and humanists. This is to say nothing of the Jews who are in a peculiar relationship to the Christian faith because we all worship the same God; yet they do not see with the same eyes as we. We have the same God, and we Christians have a New Testament faith absolutely indivisible from the Old Testament faith of the Jews. Our Lord was a Jew.

The Question of "Particularity"

What are we to make of all this and of the "scandal of particularity," as theologians call it, where all must be funneled through Jesus Christ in order to be saved and to find God?

It's not an easy question by any means, but it is a question which needs to be faced. If persons could be saved without Christ, then why should those of us who believe that God was in Christ reconciling the world unto himself pay any attention, to say nothing about making a radical commitment even unto death as Christ demands? What kind of a God is it who would populate his heaven with only a relative handful of people, those who call themselves Christians, condemning all the rest to hell whether or not they have had opportunity to respond? Are other religions valid?

It's helpful, I think, to read and study other religions, even though it's almost impossible to understand them without having faith, that is, without being on the inside rather than on the outside. Faith is educative, as we insist with our own understanding of God. It is only by faith that God can be known. Therefore, faith has something of the same meaning to people in other religions. It's only by having their faith that you can understand what they understand. We need to recognize our limitations in this regard before we make any judgments. Yet it is interesting to study other religions, and we should meet as many people as we possibly can who are devout in other faiths so that we can see their faith as more than a mere abstraction in a book, see it, rather, personified in a person who eats, drinks, loves, and hates much as we do.

Insights into the Problems of "Particularity"

There are certain insights which help us to live with this difficult question of "particularity"; the insights are not solutions but a lamp unto our feet as we try to find our way through the maze of this seeming injustice.

It is superficial and naive to say that one religion is as good as another and we're all going to the same place. Any fool can see that religions are very different, result in different social behavior, and have different meaning to the individual who has the faith in question. On the other hand, we have no way of knowing the details of heaven other than in the certainty that God will have the victory and we shall be his in perfect fellowship one day, no matter how things appear now. So we resist being naive, and yet we know little in detail.

But we can see our God in a biblical way, which will shed considerably more light than many Christians suppose.

First, you'll remember that the promise of God, the Covenant with Abraham, the call to which Abraham responded in such profound and honest trust, was that all peoples of the world would be blessed. We do not have a parochial God. The God of the Jews, often accused of being very parochial and narrow, was a God who had created all of the nations. He had created all of the earth. There was nothing beyond his reach, nothing beyond his creative and sustaining power. So we're dealing with a God of the cosmos, not a God of a single nation. The nation was only a means to an end. The end was the blessing, mind you, of the entire world. So we have a God who in his moving out is moving not only toward the old Israel or the new Israel (the Christian church) but also to the entire world. All of the world is subservient to his domination and his irrevocable plan of redemption, which is anything but narrow. Jesus said, "Other sheep have I" (see John 10:16).

The second thing we need to remember is that God shows himself in many ways. In the Old Testament he spoke through prophets; he spoke through the law; he spoke through the priesthood. Christians believe that he was alive in his Word, Jesus Christ. Further, the church has always believed, and this is not a stray thought or on the fringes, that God was in Pentecost and that everything is ultimately dependent on his Spirit. God is Spirit as well as Father and Son, Creator and Sustainer as well as Provider and Judge.

To say that God is less than Spirit is to commit a serious heresy. So the Spirit, God the lover, who came and created the church, who brought the "church social" into existence, is also the God of creation and God of the universe, the God who is over all and without whom nothing was made. The fact that he was also in Jesus Christ does not limit him but, rather, sharpens our awareness and our view of him, and yet it does not narrow him.

The same God who was in Jesus Christ is also the Holy Spirit. The Holy Spirit is also God the Creator and Father. So when we use the "name" of Jesus Christ as the funnel, we are also talking about the "name" of God the Holy Spirit. You can't have one without the other without getting into great theological difficulty. Much of our anxiety over this "scandal of particularity" is created because we tend to think of Jesus as being less than God, less than the Holy Spirit, or, perhaps more often, think of the Holy Spirit as less than Jesus.

When we use the word "name" in the biblical sense, we have to remember that it is more than just a moniker. It's more than just saying, "Oh, he's a cute little boy. Let's call him Bruce." A name was a reflection of character; it was an indication of the personality of the individual to whom the name was given. Much is made in the Bible of "God's name," not because we need a cute little "handle," as the C.B.ers say, but because we want to proclaim his character when we

73

say his name. So when we say no one shall be saved except in the name of Jesus, we are saying that no one will be saved except by the power and character of God, the God who is not only the Father and Son but also the Spirit.

John has something very interesting to say in the third chapter of his "story" about the Spirit and the necessity of being born again. We need to be born again, without question, born of the Spirit of God, and that Spirit blows where it will. It blows as the wind—it comes and it goes, and no one can control it. To me this means that there is no way we can control the saving grace of God, the Spirit which is a lover of souls, which goes out and causes people to be born again.

We have to be very careful not to bog down in verbalisms. Sometimes we imagine that we are God and that we are able to sort the good and the bad, the saved and the unsaved according to what we hear with our little pink ears. But anybody, including the devil, can speak. Verbalisms, words which we hear, are no proof of anything one way or the other. We cannot judge the wind. We cannot judge God's Spirit; we cannot be sure at any time just where the great loving heart of God is going to go or wander or what it's going to do.

Our understanding of God is limited, even though we have Jesus Christ, the Son and the great Clue. The death on the cross was not only for us but also for all those who are willing to hear and to see and to respond to the touch of God's Spirit.

It is dangerous if not heretical to try to confine the Spirit of God to Jesus' life in Palestine. There are many Christians who, in effect, do this, but they are skating on very thin theological ice because confining the Spirit in this way leaves us without a Lover in our own time. Take God's Spirit away from millions, and we take it away from ourselves. Jesus as a man is dead and gone.

But won't such an interpretation of the free-blowing grace of God cut down on our mission outreach? On our evangelism? I don't see why. If our evangelism is of God's Spirit, if it is the attempt of the Great Lover to increase attendance at the "church social," our missionary work and our evangelism must be by that same Spirit. Or it is nothing. There will be no conversions, no repentance, no turning to God except by God's Spirit. God's Spirit is the Spirit of the Great Lover. Thus, our efforts need to be in love. If we don't go in love, motivated by love, by a real desire to feed the hungry, to support the weak, to set those who are captive free—even as our Lord came to do—we will be going in the spirit of the devil, and the results will be very different from what God intends.

If we are motivated by some desire to make others as we are, to beat them up and drag them into the kingdom in order to satisfy our insecurities at the prospect of people being other than we are, we will not understand the Great Commission at-all. Love provides its own motivation; it reaches out to the beloved. For God the whole world is the beloved, and, therefore, those who have received anything of his love will be unable to keep it from spilling over and going out to those who are loveless. The free-blowing Spirit does not cut down on missionary and evangelistic activity but feeds it as scattered coals feed new fires. The fact that our mission and evangelistic work is often a burden is only an indication of our denseness, not an indication of God's lack of love.

God's love is uncontrollable and unlimited. There is no place to hide. Francis Thompson called God's Spirit the "Hound of Heaven."

It is always an odd thing to find that Christians who without the free love and grace of God would themselves be lost—"If thou, O Lord, shouldst mark iniquity, who should stand?" said the psalmist (see Psalm 130:3)—still resent the possibility that God's grace might be known in ways which have never occurred to them. Christians who seem to get a perverse delight out of the prospects of others going to hell are a contradiction. I have a lot of trouble with the old Isaac Watts' hymn: "What bliss will fill the ransomed souls/Where they in glory dwell/To see the sinner as he rolls/In quenchless flames of hell." Part of the resistance to any thought that all people will be saved is a concern with justice. If all will by some power of God's grace be saved, what motivation would we have to belong to God, to respond to his call, to be "good"? Without arguing about the obvious challenge to repent, which was in Jesus' ministry, with the threat of being cast out on the town trash fire, we need to ask ourselves if fear of hell is ever a godly motivation for being God's people. Is not the Lover motive enough to make us loving in turn? And if we are lovers in response to the Great Lover, if persons found and knew love, would there be any evil which would prevail against it? What murders, what rapes, what meanness, what greed, what gates of hell could prevail against the love of God in Christ and in the free-blowing Spirit? As for being "good," forget it. Righteousness, rightness with God, is the point, and that is the gift of God. The Pharisees were good, but they were not righteous.

Somehow, God himself was in that cross, demanding impossible **75** justice and at the same time paying the price. In his Son his Spirit was at work to do what he wanted from us because we could not possibly do it for ourselves. If one of us had died there, it would have been no different from the millions of persons, good persons, through history who have died. Ordinary death, even heroic death, would have provided nothing remedial at the center of the universe's wickedness. We are just a part of all that sin. But when the ultimate love of the Lord of life confronts death and evil, it stays confronted; and when it was defeated in the resurrection, it stayed defeated, first by Christ, Paul argues (see 1 Corinthians 15:23), but then by all those who come after in Christ, which is to say, in the Spirit. Another mystery. But there is no question about the searching love, following, seeking, and certainly finding.

11

Church Fights

By now we've seen that God is a just God. Not only does he love us, but he also will not let us fall short of his goal for us. He wants us to be perfect as he is perfect: perfect lover, perfect fellowship, perfect in our peace and grace, greeting one another with a holy kiss. How does all of this fine theory tie into the reality of church life where squabbling and fussing seem ever-present and inevitable?

The world is full of estrangement, ugliness, war and hatred, divorce, racism, sexism, ignorance and poverty, and hunger in the midst of plenty. All of these are signs that the world is far from where God wants it to be. What does this mean for us in the church?

We must keep coming back to the Covenant made with Abraham, the great promise to the world. God will not be thwarted in that promise. He will redeem, and we will respond either as John or Judas. There will be a response, and there's no way for us to avoid it. The pressure toward right and justice is inexorable and cannot be turned aside.

Thus, we encounter the other side of love. We think of it as wrath, but it is simply love unanswered; love which presses us when we don't want to be pressed, which insists on a level of behavior when we don't want to behave. God insists on love where we in our sin prefer estrangement. God brings light to the damp, warm darkness to which we have become so accustomed, which we consider to be home.

When we talk about church fights, usually we mean factions arguing over what color to paint the men's room in the new church. Churches seldom split and divide over anything important. The sixties were the exception when many churches all but split over involvement in the antiwar or civil rights movement. In the early seventies the churches split over whether or not the charismatics were in the Holy Spirit or in the human spirit. These are indeed important issues, and in some ways fighting over those issues is an improvement over some of the things over which the church has divided itself through the years. In any event, church fighting is inevitable. It is the righteous fighting of God's people against the forces of darkness and evil in the world in order to bring all the world out into the light so that it can bask in grace and peace. So our challenge is to make church fights creative and "faithful."

One of the first and most important things which needs to be done by the people of God, the church, just because they are the people of God, is to gather and praise his name. Praise is beyond reason, as we saw with Job; it shapes us by the very experience, as we saw with the psalmist; and it calls forth from us a commitment to transcendence, as it did in Abraham. Worship is the reason for which we have been created—to glorify and praise God. Nothing is more important than confronting ourselves and the world around us with our singing praises. Mere spoken words or arguments will not do. Worship is how we get our nourishment and how we retain our balance and sanity in this world.

But worship will never be worship if it does not issue in a church fight with the forces of evil in the world and in the church.

If only the battle were clearly seen, I'm sure many of us would find the courage, be inspired by God and blessed by his Spirit to go out and do battle. But the devil is not so easily dealt with. He's not going to give us clear-cut evils. He's not just going to let us use our heads. As we have seen in earlier sections of this book, theology is never merely thinking things through. It ends up dealing with mystery, mystery which absorbs us into itself. Our faith is in a personal God who is known personally.

But persons are mysterious and difficult to deal with. If only our salvation didn't have to do primarily with love. If it had mostly to do with justice, we'd be so much happier because we wouldn't necessarily have to deal with persons. We could make a case, argue it, and let the judge decide. But the quality of mercy is not strained; it falls like gentle dew from heaven. The grace and mercy of God, the love of God, goes out even to those who are wrong, precisely to those who are adjudged evil under the "law." That sort of messes us up because the devil constantly tries to convince us that we humans can build our own Towers of Babel, climb to the heavens and make judgments about right and wrong, and live comfortably ever after. We worship, and we judge. All so simple. Why argue and fight?

Unfortunately, the war we need to fight is a practical day-to-day battle with persons who are neither black nor white but rather gray, even as we are gray, struggling constantly to bring something more of the rule of God, the kingdom of God on earth. In other words, to fulfill the Covenant first given to Abraham—i.e., that God through us would bless the entire world—we must struggle even to understand, to say nothing of taking a costly stand.

Let's take several issues merely by way of illustration. We will come to no conclusions because none is entirely satisfying. I shall try to show the difficulties and the ambiguities of the issues, bringing to bear something of what we learned through our thinking about Christ the Clue and God the Humanizer, even as he works now as the Lover.

Abortion

What a difficult if not impossible issue! Christians must be engaged with this issue because it involves life and death, because it involves our understanding of women and their biology, because it involves responsibility to the medical profession which must be involved in the abortion procedures. All these are concerns of God.

It is one thing to discuss the issue of abortion as an abstract theological and philosophical matter but quite another to realize that certain positions, righteously taken, will in practice put women, especially poor women, who by their very poverty are close to the heart of a God who sides with the powerless, into alleys and backrooms for filthy coat-hanger abortions. This situation may have little to do with theory, but that's the reality whether we like it or not. It could force us into a pro-abortion position, but then again there are those other considerations with which we must also deal.

God is the Creator of life. He's on the side of life. Conceiving a child follows God in the very act of creation. Conception not only promises a new mind and a new person but also a spirit which will ultimately be able to respond to God's Spirit, a person in the image of God. In a sense to kill is to snuff out the image of God, a course which should give us great pause. Thus, the moral issue appears clear enough: we should be against all abortions.

79

But there is another strain of concern in any consideration of abortion. Is God unqualifiedly and always on the side of biological life? It would not seem so when we read about Jesus' attitude. He calls to us to take up his cross and to follow and, if necessary, to die.

Though our bodies die, our spirits cannot be touched by the forces of evil and adversity. Jesus thereby puts more stress on eternal life and the spirit than he does on mere physical life in the body. Obviously, Jesus saw his rootage in his Father and his Father's heaven rather than in this life which day by day degenerates until finally we die. The teaching of Paul and Jesus, to say nothing about the Old Testament, is that we have indeed conquered death. Thus, death is not absolute, which would seem to mean that mere biological life is also not absolute. Many will be called to die in the interest of God's purposes, even as Jesus himself died as a young man at the peak of his powers. So we tone down our absolute commitment to life itself in order to understand that there are some things more important, such as faith, commitment, and love. We would be willing to die for our families, for loved ones, for our country. God died for his enemies. We are not called to less. To be consistent, opposition to killing through abortion should lead us to oppose all killing in war or through capital punishment. Seldom is this the case, perhaps because of simple inconsistency, but then again, maybe killing cannot always be viewed in the same way.

Another aspect of the whole abortion issue concerns the soul of the mother. We use soul hesitatingly because we don't want to get into the unbiblical idea that the soul floats around quite apart from the body. There is a unity of body, soul, spirit, and mind in the Bible, but for purposes of discussion, let's talk about the spirit, or the soul, as that part which knows God as Lover or which rejects God's love.

For a group of doctors, priests, or judges to decide what a woman should do with something happening in her own body takes away her opportunity to answer God for herself. It robs her of her soul. This makes her a puppet or automaton; it erases the image of God in her. You can't love God unless you can also hate God. You can't love or hate if other people are going to decide what you should do in response to important questions. Hence, she can't be saved because she can't be lost. If she can't choose, she can't be blamed or blessed.

We have treated women as if they were biological machines dominated by men, whether it be their husbands, their fathers, or doctors, judges, and priests. Thus, the woman's right to choose, even if she chooses wrongly, is a profound spiritual matter.

Without a doubt the Bible teaches reverence for life, a superior attitude toward death, an insistence on free, moral choice; the image of God in a person is that which enables him or her to hear and to know God.

Further, we must have some sympathy for those doctors who perform with some scientific objectivity the tasks which society assigns them. Nevertheless, doctors' consciences are involved at many points. Suppose they, listening to God for themselves, disagree with the judges, the priests, and perhaps even the women who want abortions. They can send the women to other doctors, obviously, but that doesn't really resolve the problem except in a practical way. The problem of their moral choices remains even as it remains for the mothers.

So all these things together need to be considered, and it is only by prayer and by an acute listening for God the Lover that we will be able to do the loving thing. It should be obvious that simplistic clarity or judgment and condemnation must come very slowly.

Capital Punishment

Here, again, is a controversial fight into which the church must enter because so many things close to the heart of God are involved in this issue.

Again, though we believe God creates and values life, we cannot make life the ultimate value. It may be that some will have to die for a higher good. It has always been so, and those who believe in an eye for an eye and that criminals should be murdered when they in turn have murdered would agree that life is not the supreme value but, rather, justice and punishment.

A deeper spiritual issue, however, the one to which God's lovers will respond, is the insistence of God that he is Lord of life and able and willing to provide the redemption people need. His covenant and his promise are based on his ability to deliver. When Jesus is called the Logos of God in the first four verses of John's Gospel, he is being called the mind and power of God. That is, when God speaks, it is not as it is when we speak. God's word and God's accomplishment are one and the same. He does what he says he will do. He says that he will redeem and that he will provide the way.

When we assume the judgment that a person's life should be snuffed out, we are playing God. We are saying, in effect, that God's redemption is not possible for this evil person. We become the eye of God and the judgment of God and, in effect, make light of God's ability to redeem even a murderer and a rapist. We usurp his 81 authority, which is hardly the way to make love, hardly the way to respond to God's tenderness for us, hardly the way to respond to the fact that we were as filthy rags when he came to us, loved us, and redeemed us.

Sexism

This fight seems relatively new, or at least it is coming into being as one of the major focuses of the coming decade for God's people. Here, again, the issues are most complex. Each side claims that God's will and their views are one and the same.

It should be obvious that there are biological differences between boys and girls. These differences seem to be God's norm, at least as far as procreation and conceiving children are concerned. Very few people would argue about this, although various new ethical dilemmas are being introduced into this particular fight. For instance, women are being artificially inseminated, sometimes with the seed of a loved one, sometimes a stranger, bearing children without the benefit of sexual relationships with a male. The development of a fetus in a test tube, quite apart from the mother, after the egg is fertilized, seems to raise all kinds of other questions about what the male-female norm is. But for the most part a sperm and an egg are still needed to produce a fetus. The distinctions between male and female remain, and it would seem they are very much in the will of God.

Boys are boys and girls are girls, and as long as we're going to have a future for the world, it would appear to be the will of a loving God that we procreate, multiply, and replenish the earth. (Of course, replenishing is a problem all its own as we'll see in the next section under poverty.)

But the difference in the male-female genitalia do not seem to be enough to determine how we shall live our lives. We are more than our sex organs. We have minds and spirits, and we are able, if not commanded by God, to love one another, be we male or female. That is, it would seem that God wants us to love other men if we are men, and other women if we are women, and that we are all to love one another. We can, I think, especially for the sake of argument, set aside sexual relationships for the time being. Love is not limited to sex, and sex is not limited to love. Nor are sexual roles limited to genital experience. Therefore, we can set the question of sexuality aside by saying that genital contact should be responsible and loving. But love is an experience which is far greater than any genital sexuality. The problems of love remain.

The homosexuality question, so volatile and which results in such angry fighting in the church, must either be judged to be solely a genital sexual question or a question of people who make commitments to others of the same sex in the interest of love.

82

Jesus had friends of both sexes. It would seem that God loves males and females equally and expects us so to love one another. We can condemn genital sexuality between persons of the same sex without reservation and still have to deal with the problem of people who do not marry in the conventional sense but who love each other and want to share their lives. The church has always accepted women living together, or men living together, or even men and women living in communal relationships where genital sexuality did not enter into their love and relationships.

Poverty

A great part of the world is poor, so poor that it is literally dying for want of nourishment. That would be bad enough if there were not an added theological question. Another part of the world, a very small part, makes the situation even worse because it is incredibly rich. It spends most of its time trying to lose the fat that it gains by overeating. What it can't stuff in its gullet, it throws away. All this while children's bellies are bloated as they die in the streets. No scene could disturb God more.

Further, is God's creation unable to contain all the people born into it? Some are saying this is the case, and a great theological battle emerges in terms of birth and death control. Modern science, generally an instrument of God for good, compounds the problem by prolonging life and making the globe that much more crowded. People, with or without God's blessing, have sexual intercourse, conceive, and bear children, according to their "nature." Is "nature" the factor which should determine how people behave? Has God's will been so revealed in his natural creation that just by doing what comes naturally we can be sure of doing the will of God?

Or is "nature" fallen, needing God's people to share the covenant, showing how nature needs to be redeemed, changed, and brought under God's domination, just as persons are?

If we agree that the world's resources—energy to cook our food and to heat our homes, food itself, water, and other resources—are limited, then it would seem that the basic question centers around population control and the conservation of resources. The ingenuity and intelligence that God has given us become spiritual instruments to be used to excise that which is evil and to bring healing to that which is good. In any case, action by God's people must be taken.

But there is a related problem. Not all of God's people are convinced that God's creation cannot support more people, in fact many more millions of people, if resources are rightly cultivated and

83

husbanded. So they oppose population control as not being the answer, and they urge a different course of action under God.

And there is still a third question which needs to be considered: the question of distribution. With millions and millions of dying poor and millions who are gluttonously rich, distribution becomes a highly charged church fight. If the world's wealth could be equitably distributed, might we then be able to live as God's people, loving one another, caring for one another, each with a warm home and sufficient food to eat?

But all of these issues, raised here simply as problems rather than solutions, show how complex the will of God for the world is. What are we to do when we the people of God cannot agree on the will of God? The complexity of these and similar issues cannot scare us off, cannot keep us from the fight, because God's love moves out without a doubt, without letting up, and we are called to be covenant bearers to the world. At times such a pursuing God seems like a great burden. But properly understood and wrestled with, this redeeming love is as burdensome as sails are to a ship or wings to a bird.

12

Who Says So?

Precisely because religion is such a personal matter, because it transcends that which we can see, feel, and measure, the question of authority becomes critically important. Because God is personal, must we believe that there is no right which is right always and for everybody? Or wrong always?

Religious people, including Christian people, have answered the question of authority in many ways. Some of these solutions represent legitimate struggles; some are solutions worse than the problem; some become mere reflections of our sinful human condition and are of little value in understanding the will of God.

There is in every human being a lust for certainty. It's just part of our human nature. The beginning of any discussion of authority is to recognize that this dependency is there. We talked about this earlier in our discussion of God and our relationship to him, but we must come back to it now as in any discussion of authority. Upon whom or what can we depend for the will of God? "Who says so?" is a critical question.

On the surface the answer would seem obvious enough. All religion comes by revelation. This is especially true of the God of our Scriptures, who takes initiative (as we've already established), who calls his people, follows them, reaches out to them, forgives them, and generally pursues them even beyond death. So then, what's the problem? If this God is so bent on making himself known to us, there should be little difficulty in agreeing one and all as to just what he demands from us.

But it's not quite that simple. For whatever reason, God is personal and has made us personal in his own image; his revelation comes in and through people. Even our Scriptures were written by people; albeit spirit-filled people, people nevertheless. Scriptures were not "automatic writing"; they were written by people who had lived, responded to God, and had their own personalities merged with the Holy Spirit in the preaching of their particular message.

Some find this distressing. They would prefer a Scripture found under a rock or lowered from heaven on a rope, written in some language which would be impressive to the entire world. I had a friend in seminary who was from Brooklyn and who could never understand why God had to špeak to the Jews in that difficult Hebrew language. Why couldn't he have revealed himself in Brooklynese? My friend did not have any appreciation of how difficult it was for the rest of us to understand him. We preferred to wrestle with the Hebrew. Why could God not speak in some totally original language, which would be beyond dispute and debate, free from any ethnic or local interpretation? But God, however, chose to reveal himself in a Person and in a people. His ultimate Word to us was in Jesus, whom we came quickly to call the Christ.

Jeremiah, one of the great prophets of the Old Testament, with his close relationship to God, which is common to all the prophets, predicted (31:31-34) that someday there would be a new Covenant, one not written on cold tables of stone but written in the heart, in the brown eyes of a peasant, to be apprehended in love rather than duty. This new Covenant, to which Jesus made reference at the Last Supper, was to be different from the old in that it would be internal, spiritual, not local but universal. It would be known in the heart, knowledge directly from God, with no intermediary, no priest, perhaps not even a teacher (see Jeremiah 31) necessary. There will be no necessity for the scholar, for the priest, for anyone who holds secret knowledge or who has a corner, as it were, on the truth.

Without minimizing the law or the old Covenant with Abraham, or with Noah before him, God was to improve on our human condition; he would show himself so that all persons, anyone who could love, could know him. Anyone with a heart can have a new Covenant with God. They needn't be Jews, ethnically speaking; they don't need to be from a certain part of the world or be a certain color or belong to a certain class. The new Covenant would truly be the blossom of the old Covenant. The old Covenant with the Jews was for the blessing of the world; the new Covenant would be grasped by the world.

This is a remarkably heartening promise and was fulfilled for our redemption in Jesus of Nazareth. We praise God for a personal Savior and delight in a personal relationship to God.

If this is true, and I profoundly believe it is, then why do we constantly lust after certainty other than the certainty of God's love in Christ? Why do we need more than love to answer the question "Who says so?" Love says so. But—we do need more. All religious people do. At the slightest provocation we turn from God's new Covenant, written in the heart, to covenants written in stone, in a book, by a dictator, or in certain procedures of the church which are generally called sacraments. The fact that Baptists call them ordinances doesn't alter the veneration which church people pay to these procedures. They are the ones which "administer" the way, the answer.

If we find authority which is delegated to an institution unsatisfactory, the question "Who says so?" remains a primary one for us.

One answer would seem to be, "Jesus says so." But what all did Jesus say? In John's Gospel, there is reference to the many, many things which Jesus said and did about which we have no record. As we'll see in a moment when we discuss the Scriptures, the Gospel accounts are all filtered through the eyes of the writers, under the leadership of the Spirit to be sure, but with distinct purposes. The purpose serves as a filter so that extraneous material is not introduced to confuse the primary thrust of the Gospel account in question. In a sense, we know relatively little about Jesus. He wrote nothing himself except some scratching in the sand. Sand soon is blown smooth by the winds. Is anything less durable than writing in the sand? Was God telling us something when he had Jesus live rather than write, heal rather than philosophize, confront rather than speculate?

At various times in history, Jesus has been known as the Great Teacher. Who says so? The Great Teacher says so, that's who. Yet it's hard to understand how he got that title since he taught relatively little which was new. He was himself new, bringing a new promise and a new Covenant. But the power of the New Testament is not in any new theology or teaching but, rather, in the Person who had in him somehow the very authority and power to forgive sins. That is why he was murdered. It was not a question of what was said but, rather, his answer to the question "Who says so?" Jesus answered, "My Father and I say so." But that authority, that certainty—the faith of Jesus in the Father—was a matter of relationship, a relationship which he wanted to cause in all of his disciples (see John 17). Thus, for Jesus religious certainty was a matter of love, faith, relationship, and unity of spirit with the Father, not of teaching per se.

Love, faith, relationship: these are all subjective words. By subjective we mean they exist inside us. We ourselves are the subject of the sentence, as it were. We act upon an object which is beyond and outside the subject. God is the Great Subject; we are also subjects because we are in his image. God takes initiative and acts on the object; we take initiative and act on objects. Our initiative, our will, our purpose are all things within us rather than outside where they can be seen and measured by others. Others can see the "fruit" of our motives, our values, our intentions, but they can never be sure that they have seen the real thing. This is why Jesus said that judgment was wrong. Not only is judgment itself wrong in spirit, but also we are incapable of judging a person's subjective or inside motives, and it, therefore, is wrong because it is impossible.

Precisely because these very important matters of faith and love and judgment are inside, are subjective, we are left with less than a measurable, touchable certainty upon which everyone can agree.

Subjectivity is hard to manage. This is true of our own subjectivity as well as the subjectivity of others. The heart is a fickle thing. Love is used to describe many feelings and emotions which are merely greed or lust. So we're sort of stuck with one another, unable to judge one another with any certainty and yet with God and each other as our primary means of knowledge. The question "Who says so?" is answered by persons, each of whom is in a sense a light unto himself or herself.

It's not hard to understand, therefore, why Christians in various ages have tried to find other supports or backup systems as the means to the establishment of God's kingly rule. Let's take a look at some of the ways in which the church has tried to answer the question "Who says so?" the question of authority.

Conscience

Some have tried to stay very close to the meaning of what we've been saying about persons being the judge of their own feelings. They have made the conscience, or the "inner light," in each person the primary authority. The Society of Friends actually uses the term "inner light" to describe the conscience, that subjective power within each person, the ability to choose and to decide and to know what God is saying. You'll remember that when we talked about the prophets, we said that in prophetic persons—such as Isaiah, Jeremiah, Amos, Micah—the knowledge that they had a word from

God written in their bones and their heart was very much a part of their authority. In other ways, of course, the Society of Friends and others who stress conscience would be very different from the prophets. But it should not be lost on us that though the Society of Friends is a very small group, it has had a long and noble history as a sharp, prophetic edge in our society, going up against power and the establishment in the interest of justice, peace, and other matters pertaining to the quality of life to all peoples. There is a connection with the prophets there somewhere.

Baptists have been in that same tradition. They make a great deal of the amount of water they use to baptize, but the real pivotal truth of the Baptists in their beginnings was that they wanted to have direct access to the Holy Spirit. They wanted to answer the question "Who says so?" with their own consciences. enlightened by the direct Spirit of God. They wanted no bishop, no prayer book, no liturgy between them and God's Spirit. Therefore, only adults were admitted to the church and people one could reasonably assume to have the ability to make a mature response to God's Spirit and God's leading, a response not allowed the immature or the child.

This particular interpretation of authority has been a powerful instrument for liberty and freedom for all peoples in any culture or time when people who believe in conscience have been prominent and even at times when they have not. But we also need to look at some of the problems that a great amount of stress on conscience presents to us.

The story is told of the pastor who was having a run-in with his board of deacons. They argued for hours, the preacher on one side and the deacons on the other. Finally, the pastor said that he felt they should adjourn for fifteen minutes to pray. After fifteen minutes the meeting was convened, and the pastor announced that he had prayed and that God had agreed with him.

I must stress over and over again that we remain sinners. Thus, in all our considerations about God we must remember that our hearts are corrupt. The shrewdest work of the devil is to take the very highest which we desire and turn it into the lowest. Our desire for God can be very easily turned into idolatry as we invariably set up a definition and understanding of God which suits our own proud and lustful purposes. We must always be on our guard. Though we hold our conscience high, we must at the same time recognize the need for a corrective. So to hold the conscience as the primary source of authority, the answer to the question "Who says so?", is not by itself enough.

The Bible

Others, recognizing the tendency to self-centeredness in this emphasis on conscience, feel the need for an outside or objective touchstone. They want authority placed other than just in conscience. For Protestants, those churches which came into being in the 1500s in reaction to the corruption in the Roman Catholic Church of that time, have answered this need with heavy reliance on the Scriptures.

It would be hard to emphasize Scriptures too much, so important are they. But just as conscience can be emphasized to a fault, Scriptures have been stressed to the point where they have replaced God as the object of worship. There can be no transcendence in a book, per se. The Scriptures (to give life to an object) would be horrified to find that instead of pointing to God and Christ, they were pointing to themselves. That is, the Bible teaches us a great deal about God and about Christ. It teaches us very little about itself. The Bible is alive because the same Spirit which confronted the people who wrote the Bible is still confronting us. Their experiences in a deep sense are also our experiences, made lively and real for us by the Spirit which is neither the past nor future but always present, the Spirit of the God who calls himself, "I Am."

In an age when science has been riding high and, until the last decade, without much opposition, it is understandable that those who believe in God with all their hearts, minds, souls, and spirits would want to have something comparable with which to fight against science. Science delivered the world from superstition, subjectivity, claims which couldn't be proved or demonstrated, claims at odds with the evidence. The evidence is available, says science, to anyone who has the nerve to look for it, to seek it out, to organize it, and to "prove" whatever is claimed. But for many years no one raised questions about those areas of life which cannot be demonstrated or proven "scientifically," which, nevertheless, are absolutely important and essential to any living human being. And instead of raising that question themselves, the church ofttimes merely tried to do battle with science on scientific grounds, attempting to give the Bible a scientific meaning which the Bible never intended, doesn't have, and, more to the point, doesn't need for its authority. The Bible is about God, God who is immeasurable and beyond our complete understanding. Christian faith is not opposed to science, not in the sense as has often been thought: that is, as the enemy of science. Rather, the faith is about transcendence, about that which is beyond the province of science, beyond measurement, and beyond the laboratory. There are no cross purposes. The Bible envelops science as one of those ways in which God would have us know the truth. Science can explore, investigate, measure, gather its facts, and the people of God can say, "Amen." We have no need to fear what science will find because science must always work within the confines of God's creation. If science gets outside the confines of the physical creation, it no longer is science, but becomes philosophy and religion.

When religion tries to meet science on its own ground, that is, to produce physical evidence which will support without a doubt the beliefs of a group of religious people, it corrupts itself as well as the Scriptures. The argument about the infallibility of the Scriptures or their inerrancy still rages. The people who engage in that battle are well meaning, but it gets us nowhere and creates immense stumbling blocks for people who would otherwise be drawn to Christ. Only God is inerrant and infallible.

The question put by the people who believe in the scientific infallibility of the Scriptures is, "What shall be our authority if it is not the Bible?" My answer, as well as the answer of many millions of Christians, is God himself. God is alive and he reveals himself; he meets us at our conscience and in our world, just as he did Abraham and Isaac and Jacob, the prophets, and the Pharisees and Sadducees of Jesus' time, for that matter. To make anything other than God our authority is idolatry. Protestants who have rebelled against the human pope have tried to make a paper pope out of the Bible. Whether a human pope or a paper pope, idolatry is nevertheless idolatry.

None of this is to minimize the importance of Scriptures as the touchstone against which we measure our consciences and our personal experiences with God. The spirit which is our authority is the Spirit of God. That sounds dumb, but it's an important statement. If the Spirit which we claim is inconsistent with the Spirit which confronted Abraham, Job, or Isaiah, we should be profoundly suspicious. The one who confronts us must be consistent with the one who confronted those in ancient times. Therefore, if God speaks to me and tells me to pick up a hatchet and hit you in the head, dear reader, you could conclude, with a high degree of certainty, that it is not the Spirit of God speaking to me, at least not the God who was one with Jesus. Now this gets tricky because there were people in the Old Testament who heard God say bizarre things. Abraham and the order to sacrifice Isaac is a case in point. But we go to Jesus for our clue, as I argued in the first section of this book, and the Clue becomes very enlightening to our conscience. That Clue is given to us in a profound sense in the Scriptures. The answer to the question "Who says so?" therefore becomes a two-pronged answer: our conscience says so, but our conscience is checked against the Scriptures.

I will return to a consideration of the Bible in chapter 13. For now, we see the Bible as one part of the three sources of authority for the Christian.

The Church

There is yet a third checkpoint which we need to recognize in attempting to establish religious authority. This is what we call the church, or tradition. I'm tentative about defining the church as such because tradition means many different things. Further, the church was not clearly defined by Jesus as an institution. It came into existence not so much by plan as in reaction to the presence of God in his Spirit at Pentecost when God poured himself out on his people. A great unity, a great reversal of the Tower of Babel, took place. The people understood one another. That communion was the mark of God's presence in the world; there was unity where before there had been estrangement. The apostle Paul, the church's first great organizing theologian, makes unity the key to knowing the Spirit of God. Where the Spirit is, there will be love and unity; those who were far off will be brought nigh. (See Ephesians 4 or all of First Corinthians.)

As we've already indicated, the Spirit of God is a Lover, empowering us to love one another. Loving one another is called the church, an intimacy which the apostle Paul describes by using the body as an illustration. How much more intimate can you get than your hand with your foot or your eye with your ear, each one dependent upon the other for its very existence?

Thus, in a sense the church is not a human plan. It's not a structure designed by human beings, but it is, rather, the gift of God, the by-product and the creation of God himself. God generated it in the first place and continues to generate and sustain it.

It's important that we understand that the church is the creation of God's Spirit and not of our own making. We have our discussions, our business meetings, and make our decisions quite often on the basis of whether or not it is good business or good manners or something else taken from our culture rather than understanding that the church is not defined by human wisdom or merit. Rather, it is shaped by the love of God which goes out to all persons and all people who have only one thing in common: the word of God in Jesus Christ and in the Spirit.

In a sense, then, the church is as Paul described it—the body of Jesus Christ and an extension of God's incarnation in Jesus. Jesus died, rose again by the power of God, and will return in the consuming glory of God. But in the meantime Jesus is gone. The authority has been replaced on earth by his disciples who are bonded in his own intimate, loving Spirit. They continue through the centuries and through the years as the presence of God to one another.

It is easy to see, even for Protestants, that the traditions of this body we call the church become through the centuries very important. The church is a living organism even as the human body is alive. As a body responds to its environment, skin to the sun, the internal organs to the heat or cold, so the church has responded to its environment throughout history. It has not always responded properly, even as we don't always respond properly in our bodies. We stay in the sun far too long or go out without proper clothing and catch cold. The church as a body has also responded poorly at times; yet it nevertheless has remained the body of Christ.

At times the church as a body has responded to its environment in an attempt to protect itself from the cold of various ungodly forces, sometimes from the heat of unfriendly governments, or from the snow and rain of conflicting philosophies. In order to keep itself safe and pure, to protect itself or to make itself healthy, it has tried to set up protections and safeguards. The church has sincerely attempted to keep channels open and clear for the grace of God, which gives life to the church, the power for mission, evangelism, and the redemption of the world.

Some of these channels are called sacraments. Baptists in the Western Hemisphere have been nervous about using that word, though it's used by English and European Baptists. We prefer the word "ordinance," though that always reminds me of a cannon (and I don't mean canon). Whatever we call them, there are procedures traced back to the life of Jesus which are practiced in the church through the centuries in order to keep the Spirit of God alive in our midst. Some churches have several sacraments (the Roman Catholic, seven; the Episcopalians, five; the Baptists, Presbyterians, and Methodists, two). Though Baptists are supposedly in the "free church" tradition, they are seldom less rigid about observance of the Lord's Supper and baptism than are the highly liturgical churches which treat sacraments as the most sacred of practices. Just because we claim to be in a free church tradition does not make us less rigid about our liturgy. Because our liturgy is more simple does not mean it is not liturgy, nor does it mean that it is not as rigid.

But history has shown that sacraments and channels have not been good enough to give the church a secure feeling about authority. So there grew early in the church's history an authority given over to leadership, to ministers, priests, and the various levels of administrators called elders, presbyters, and bishops in the Bible and called ministers, priests, cardinals, and popes in history. It is not surprising to find, therefore, that one of the sacraments for millions of Christians is the sacrament of ordination. The churches which have shied away from giving too much authority to the clergy, with the exception of a few denominations which have no clergy at all, still ordain with a sense of significance and importance. Authority is given to men and, increasingly in our day, to women. Though the church can be understood in its desire for control through sacrament and priest, there has been no guarantee that these safeguards themselves would not become idols with great internal danger to the church. Anytime the church has given too much authority to its clergy, there has been corruption and trouble.

Thus, the three-way test for authority: the individual conscience, the Scriptures, and the tradition of the church as it has wrestled with the issues of mission and survival through history. We should add that the church is always alive and contemporary. Therefore, issues need to be struggled with continually and anew in each generation, in the presence of fellow Christians, all seeking the Spirit of God in their consciences, and turning to the Scriptures for insight and confirmation, again, under the Spirit.

We live in a complex age with moral questions being raised all about us such as have never been raised before. One thinks of the emerging rights of women as individuals, the openness of the homosexual, the technical extension of life (if it is life), to say nothing about the many cults which are springing up in this time of spiritual starvation. The mainstream churches are getting weaker while cults grow stronger and compete with one another for the young. What are we to make of all of this? Who is to be the authority when a claim is made and we raise the question "Who says so?" Where do we turn for our answer?

I was visiting my dental hygienist recently and learned that she was a "lapsed" Catholic, a young person obviously well educated and sensitive, very much in the swim of things as she raises her family in these difficult times. Her remark about her experience in the church was rather startling. Though generally not at a loss for words, with her hands and tools in my mouth I was unable to speak. She was in a rare position and took advantage of it. She had left the church, she said, because the church kept changing its position on things. What good is a church that changes its mind? She was dealing in a pointed and direct way with the question of authority. She wanted a church which was unchanging, which had a corner on the truth and which would provide stability in a rapidly changing world, a world pushing and shoving and bending human beings out of shape.

It's partly the church's own fault that she left. The church has claimed for itself an infallibility which it really does not have and which has only confused people, leading them to false expectations.

By the same token, Protestants look to the Scriptures for answers to particular questions, and because those particular situations did not exist in biblical times, they assume that the Bible has no answer. So they leave the church.

Others outside the church change their consciousness and their conscience with drugs of one kind or another. They have no confidence from their normal internal feelings and ingest chemicals to produce an answer. Literally tons of books are produced helping people to deal with their feelings, which is another way of describing conscience. Remedies range from, "If it feels good, do it," to assertiveness training so you'll have enough nerve to say no to those around you, to pressures and circumstances which seem to manipulate and rob you of your strength. But the question remains, "Who says so?" When do we say, "No," legitimately, and when should we say, "Yes"? Life does not divide itself into neat little packages; many times a great no is needed, requiring a strength and conviction not easily supported by the evidence, by the culture, by the society, or anybody else, including your loved ones. Such a direction comes only from a God who is alive and acting, who can be known and checked out, as it were, with a historical record which we call the Scriptures and with the lives of millions of people who are sensitive to the same godly issues, whom we call the church.

In the last analysis the only authority which the Christian has is the authority of God. All other authorities are semi-authorities and, as a result, cannot be trusted too far. We never really know anything for sure, and for that reason we live by faith. We are justified by our faith in God, his ability to lead us, to guide us, to forgive us, to love us, to catch us up, to set us on a solid rock. That is the only certainty there is, and any attempt to prop it up or shore it up is, ironically, to destroy it and make it into something else.

PART IV

Two Related Matters

13

The Bible Alive

In chapter 12 I held the Bible high as one of the three sources of authority for the Christian life. I don't want to minimize or confuse the point I hope I made there, but the Bible needs a bit more attention because it is so critically important and because by its very nature it can be so easily abused. Not that conscience and tradition, the other two checkpoints for authority, are not important. But the Bible has a special place. No small part of that place is the insistence, historically more by Protestants, that the Bible is a book which belongs to the people. The Reformation was due in no small part to the invention of movable type which allowed the Bible to be mass produced, as it were. No longer was the Bible to be painstakingly copied, thus possessed more or less by monks in the monastery. Such a process had made each manuscript extremely valuable, far beyond the reach of the ordinary person even if one had wanted, or had been permitted by the church, to have a copy of one's own.

God "Speaks" Through the Bible

Because of this commitment to common access to the Bible, education has been a most critical emphasis in the Protestant church and tradition. The ordinary Christian, whatever that phrase means, needed to have the education and skills to read and interpret the Bible for himself or herself.

But this brings almost as many problems in its wake as it does blessings. The Bible can be used of the very devil to prove the most dastardly things in the world. The Bible is not a dead book. It is not a collection of old sayings. It is alive. It lives by the same Spirit which first inspired it, and it must be respected as a living organism. By the same token, its life can be distorted and twisted.

We need to sit before the Bible and let it speak to us in our own day. The people and the situations may be ancient, but the God who speaks to us now is the same today, yesterday, and forever. His Word and his words have a meaning for each one in his or her situation, for any contemporary problems.

If we believe in a living God, who not only elects us and provides for us before the beginning of time and long after time is finished but who also warms our hearts moment by moment, we would not expect to resent his real presence among us. But there are those who are so sure that they know exactly what the Bible means or, better, know what the Bible means for the practical pressures they feel from their surroundings that they do not want anything added, including the presence of the living God in their midst.

To believe that God is alive and that his words are alive is a serious business, and we, like the Grand Inquisitor in *The Brothers Karamasov* might find "liveliness" most threatening.

In a moment we will look at a few of the disciplines necessary if we are to take reading the Bible seriously. But before we do that, I must make it very clear that we cannot be put off by those who would make the understanding of the Bible a mystery in the academic sense, a special knowledge owned by experts. The great biblical scholar Harnack, one of the greatest of all times, said, in effect, that the charwoman (scrubwoman) with the Bible was greater than the great Harnack without it. What he meant was that the common person, reading the Bible for himself or herself, is far better off than a person who knows a great deal about it but does not see it as "alive." Even though we must grant that a great deal of damage has been done by people who abuse the Bible, often for their own purposes, we cannot allow those risks to drive us away from the insistence that the Bible is best interpreted by the Spirit and that it must be read, on the face of it, by every Christian.

As there is snobbery in scholarship and pride in knowledge, so also there is a reverse snobbery which takes great pride in being ignorant or in not having the time to study the Bible properly.

If we could carry ourselves back to the time of Gutenbérg, the inventor of type as we know it, in the sixteenth century, we would be astounded as we think of the versions and translations of the Bible which are available to us today. To us all. Not many of us can read the Hebrew in which the Old Testament was originally written, and not many can read the Greek in which the New Testament has come down to us. But for our purposes here—not to put the rap on serious scholarship—translations are all we need. We do not use these riches in our own language nearly enough. Certainly being able to read biblical material in the original languages (the original manuscripts are not available to us—only early copies and in some cases copies which are not all that early) would be an asset.

In our day not even cost can be used as an excuse for not reading the Bible personally, not even by those of us who are most limited financially. Organizations like the American Bible Society will provide Scriptures free, if necessary. In any case, remarkable editions, beautifully bound and printed, are readily available for practically nothing. For instance, the *Good News Bible* is not only beautifully and economically published, but it is also extremely accurate.

Before I go further, perhaps I should say just a word about the difference between a translation and a paraphrase. A translation means that the materials are taken from one language to another. The translation is done on a word-to-word basis, with great care being given to find the proper word in the language into which the material is being translated. But languages don't always match up word for word, and the translator has to make some judgments. Often something is lost in strict word meaning, though not necessarily in thought meaning. When the language is as close to word for word as possible, it is called a translation. It is as literal as possible. Then again, sometimes in the interests of understanding, the original Hebrew or Greek is translated loosely, perhaps even into slang. Such a loose paraphrasing, for example, would be found in the Phillips translation of the New Testament, an extremely helpful point of comparison with the more literal translations. By their very nature, of course, paraphrases go out of fashion. I personally find the *Good News Bible,* a literal translation yet in contemporary language, the most helpful and meaningful for me. Every Christian should own a number of Bibles, ranging from very strict translations to those which are, in so far as possible, paraphrases.

Let's all deliver ourselves and those around us from the fancy Bibles which rest in all their leather and gilt splendor on the coffee table. Let's get over the reverence for the Bible as an inanimate object and see it as a living thing ready to speak and confront as well as comfort us. Mark it up, tear out its pages if you want to carry a puzzling or meaningful passage with you; paste a page on your mirror for a week to think about as you prepare for the day. Only the superstitious or those like the Grand Inquisitor, who think that the

Bible is a dead thing of the past, treat the Bible as if it were a mere object. To treat it as a fetish, or a totem—something that if treated with reverence will bring good or bad luck, something that has magic about it—is unacceptable to the Lord.

Disciplines Necessary to Read the Bible Seriously

Having said all of this and urging a lively approach to the Scripture, I must add a word regarding discipline. We are, as I hope I've demonstrated by now, limited in our ability to reason. I don't take back any of what I've said about our limitations, but I also want to be sure that we do not do less than we should to understand what we can. I reiterate that knowing what the Bible says is not all that difficult; applying it to our life situation is another matter.

There are some terms and practices every Christian should at least be familiar with, if for no other reason than that we not be pointlessly threatened as so many Christians have been by something which has been in reality a tremendous boon to Bible study; two such terms and concepts are "higher (literary) criticism" and "historical criticism."

But first maybe we need to think a bit about this word "criticism." Criticism is not as nasty as it sounds and doesn't deserve the negative image which common usage has given it. Criticism can be good as well as bad. All it means is that persons confronting the material, whatever it might be, will be as careful as they can be in the treatment of that material, that they will use whatever brains God has given them to treat the material with respect. They listen but then ask questions of clarification. The teacher who never gets criticism, in this sense, the one who lectures and then has the students passively close their notebooks and steal away is not a good teacher. After the teacher shares the information which he or she has because of disciplined study, there must be all sorts of questions, concerns about the meaning of what has been said or read for the particular students. The best students are the ones who question something until they are satisfied that they know all there is to know and can then treat the subject with a good deal more respect than if they had not made it "their own."

Higher criticism is the careful attempt to know what the writers meant by the kind of words they used to say something. It sounds complicated but really isn't. If someone walked up to you in the supermarket and said, apropos of nothing, "I am a mighty oak," apart from thinking that he was missing a few shingles, you would not conclude that he thought of himself as a tree. Usually. If you felt that the person was reasonably sane, you would immediately assume that he was speaking of his strength, those attributes we associate with the mighty oak. You would assume that he was referring in a poetic way to his sturdiness, not to his bark, leaves, or acorns. Higher criticism is often a matter of the application of common sense.

The church has raged back and forth, unnecessarily as it turns out, over any "criticism" of the Bible because of misunderstanding of the reverence implied in "criticism."

For instance, the use of myth as one form of literary expression has upset us something fierce because we assume that myth means untruth. Not at all. It could fairly be said that a myth is a way of expressing a truth which is truer than true, a truth so widely and universally true that it is too much to be contained in simple historical facts. But even if myth in the Bible is taken literally, there is little harm done if we can remember our lessons about being humble where any definition of Almighty God is concerned. Literalism can never be applied to a God beyond our ability to describe completely. But it is helpful for those who are poetic to know that there are profound poems in the Bible as well as long, sometimes dry and dusty, family histories. These two very different kinds of literature are not "thought" of in the same way. There are personal letters in the New Testament written by people who had known Jesus personally or who, like the apostle Paul, insisted that their experiences with Christ (on the Damascus road and elsewhere) were as real as knowing Jesus in the flesh. There are strange books in both Testaments, such as Revelation, which deal in images and symbols and are cryptic and hard to understand on purpose. They were in code, to be understood in the early persecuted church only by the Christians and not by their Roman tormentors. The only people who would understand the meaning of Revelation were those who already had the "code book" of Daniel and some other similiar materials. Further, there are "Gospel" accounts, each differing from the others according to what the writer was trying to say to the growing and scattered church.

Thus higher, or literary, criticism is common sense if we think a bit and if we feel free to be "critical." If you can't discern the difference, let us say, between the great hymns and testimonies commonly called the Psalms and Leviticus. then the Bible will be useless to you.

The second "tool" we must know about is "historical criticism." This criticism concerns itself, as does all of history, with "time." When were particular books written? What were the historical conditions surrounding the writing? For the Bible is not an

103

abstraction; it was written with keen regard for the pressures and forces which the people of God were facing and in which Almighty God was acting to show himself and his plan for redemption.

In the New Testament again, for instance, the fact that the letters to the Corinthians and Thessalonians were early, before the church had any of the Gospels which spell out the life of Jesus in written form, makes the meaning of those personal letters to the various local churches much more meaningful.

Unlike higher criticism, historical criticism is not as much a matter of common sense. It requires discipline and some study. Again, it is not esoteric or strange to the average Christian. Further, there are many marvelous historical and background materials available. Barclay's commentaries on the New Testament are an example.

Christians must take the Bible seriously, especially since it is alive. We would not speak lightly of discipleship; part of our stewardship must be the stewardship of the mind. The time it takes to feed our minds and to get the meanings reasonably accurate before we begin the most subtle and difficult task of applying the Word is time well spent. Reading the Bible in light of the situation in life in which we find ourselves, or perhaps reading it even more critically, must be counted among our offerings to God.

14

Priest, Preacher, or What?

We can't end any survey of theology without considering the presence of the priest. The word carries a multitude of meanings. When we think of the ancient priests of Israel, as compared to the prophets—the priests with all the careful rules and regulations which were to help the people to know and be the holy people of a holy God, and the prophets with their abrupt, passionate, blind-side approach to righteousness—we get, even back then, a hint of the wide differences in the understanding of religious leadership.

In our own time, many denominations and religious groups would not think of calling their leaders priests. Some groups are extremely folksy and informal; they call their leader "Preacherman" or even "Preach." Others, like Lutherans, with a strong ethnic tradition, are accustomed to calling their ministers "Pastor," a title which is also used by many other groups in addition to their favorite terms for their leaders. In groups like the Episcopalians, the terms "minister" and "priest" are both used freely. Of course, in the Roman and other Catholic churches, "priest" is used almost exclusively, though it is not at all uncommon to call a Roman priest "Pastor." The term "Father" is used in connection with those churches which have a high and specialized view of the ministry, in which great authority is placed with the priest to the degree where he is representative of the literal fatherhood of God.

And, of course, we must not neglect to mention those religious groups which do not recognize any one member of their congregation as being any different in authority and power than any other member.

In effect, they do not "ordain" any person to a special role of leadership, authority, or knowledge.

What the Bible Says Regarding the Ministry

What does the Bible say about leadership and ministry? Again, it will depend on how you read it. Almost every group uses the Bible as its authority for their view of the ministry. But there are a few things which seem central and relatively undebatable.

There can be no question that theology is the business of every Christian. We have assumed that in the writing of this book. The next question concerns the degree and the time and energy which can be devoted to the study of these important matters. Also, there is the matter of the functioning of the religious body, the church or the sect, in its day-to-day business. Does not someone have to have a little more expertise, a bit more time and energy to devote to those institutions which are always present when people organize for worship and service?

In the Bible, if that is relevant for today, and some of us think it is very much so, every believer was a priest. But in addition there were gifts given by God's Spirit, given to some and not to others. Some were to be evangelists, whatever that meant; some were to be teachers; some were to be healers; and some had the gift of speaking in tongues, a gift which, incidentally, the apostle Paul held to be of little value for the church as a whole.

The people within the congregations were set aside according to their obvious gifts, and they were called elders, or even bishops, along with those called deacons who served the needs of the people. But where there were gifts, they were not to be looked upon as making the persons who had them more important than persons who had other gifts. In fact, the writer of the book we call Ephesians (see 4:11ff.) makes it clear that those who have gifts are called to build up *all* the saints for the work of the ministry. The ministry belongs to all the people, and the people who are set aside have a servant function rather than a station, or position, of power. They are to build everybody up; the ministry belongs to everybody in the church.

This should give us a clue, or several for that matter. If we are to have a separate class of people called "ministers" or whatever, then they are set aside for the growth and development of the rest of the Christian people. They are not privileged except in that they are privileged to serve the rest of the Christian body. There have been times, and not all of them have been in the Middle Ages, when the clergy have completely missed the point, and somehow imagined that the church existed primarily for their comfort and support.

The meaning and import of ordination become critical even when we allow for the priesthood of the believer and even when the one set aside for ordination realizes he or she is only a servant. Many believe that when the priest is ordained, he or she thus becomes the sole administrator of the sacraments, the sacraments being the chief if not sole means of knowing and having God. The priest then becomes a necessary channel and has quite a different role from the minister who is more of an enabler or a teacher; the priest is a controller of the grace of God through the functions of the sacrament.

As we might expect, still other groups, like the Society of Friends, which have no ordained ministers (in some cases there are pastors, but that is a geographical or local phenomenon) also put little stress, if any, on sacramental observance. The Quakers, as the Friends are often called, do not even have music among their more strict adherents. Nothing external is to interfere with the working of the Spirit in the inner light which is in each believer. But it is significant also that the Quakers have traditionally had fine private schools. These schools are often related to their Meeting Houses' day-to-day functioning. For practical purposes, if not for theoretical purposes, the Quakers do have a clergy.

Baptists and others in the free church tradition—free, that is, from a rigid hierarchy of power and authority—are in between the Friends on the left and the Catholics on the right. Baptists feel that ordination is important and that the ministry is a high calling. Baptists, for the most part, at least in recent years hold that young people, men and women (some denominations feel strongly negative about female ministers, while others like the Baptists have had them for over a hundred years) should indeed be set aside in the biblical sense and trained in our graduate schools which we call seminaries. Many in the church these days insist not only on seminary training (usually three years, or four with an intern year) but also four years of undergraduate work in college prior to seminary.

Thus, in terms of time spent in preparation, the ministry has slipped downward in position historically, while many other groups have worked themselves up to the position of "professional." There was a time when the most important professionals in the community were the ministers. With the rise of science and technology and the growth of the industrial society in America as well as in Western Europe, the ministers sank in the professional rankings as they were replaced by other arbiters of public and private morals—sometimes by the physician, more recently the psychiatrist, and, oddly, in the area of service to people, by the government. Thus, the role of ministers has become unfocused; it is hard for older ministers and their congregations to know just what to expect from modern ministers. Is their primary role that of preacher, even in an age when all sorts of information is gotten every few seconds from TV? There are more TV sets in this country than indoor toilets. Is their role that of helping with the individual's spirit and mind, even as psychology and its related "sciences" grow at a tremendous rate? Is their role that of teacher, even as colleges—community and otherwise—spread like wildfire? Is their role primarily that of the business person, responsible for the smooth administration of the organization? Is that enough of a challenge for a person with an education which combines professor, scholar, psychologist, and communicator/actor?

The Place of the Religious Leader

Many of the things the church has always done are now done by the government and by other community and social agencies. The church has had a noble history in prison reform, the care of orphans and the poor, even in hospital and medical care, but the mantle for these things has passed to the secular world. What, then, is the place of the religious leader, the one who is set aside to do the work of ministry?

Just how is the minister to be defined as a professional in the manner that other professionals are clearly defined by the societies, the standards of excellence, and the preparation required for "practice"? How can the nebulous business of ministry to persons ever be evaluated so that commonly recognized standards can be held?

The expectations of the minister, and interestingly enough the priest, are alarmingly unclear. It is hard for the minister to know what is his or hers to do, who he or she is professionally, to say nothing of the people who contribute to the budget for the minister's salary and who have a right to know what they ought to be getting for their money.

As we might expect, the problem of knowing what to do is less pressing when the religious enterprise in question, be it local church or denomination, is successful. The task then becomes simply to do more of the same, whatever it is that is making the organization grow and expand.

But when biblical or theological standards are applied, then other measurements must be taken; and success, though it breeds more success, cannot stand as the primary standard. We immediately think of Jesus, whose disciples we are, who was a loser by our society's standards. He didn't suit anybody and refused to play the numbers game. At the end there was virtually no one at his side, only a few afar off. He did all the wrong things by modern public relations measurements. He sided with the wrong people, mingled with social outcasts, and insisted that the losers of this world would be in the places of honor at the kingdom banquet—indeed that they would inherit the earth. Christians who are serious about discipleship are caught between the world's definition of the professional and the standards for righteousness which Jesus himself taught and practiced and which certainly should have something important to do with the way all Christians behave, and even more certainly should have something to do with those who are set aside full-time to make theological observations and judgments about the lives we lead and the world we live in.

Jesus was clear about his values. The most important thing for him was the will of God, and we've already seen that the will of God is to bless all the people in the world. People are the point. For ministry, professional or otherwise, the function of the people of God is other people: their well-being, their care, in short, their salvation.

We live in a society which does not hold those same values. The purpose of society is said to be the good of its citizens, and in theory this may well be true. Societies form themselves for mutual protection and advancement. But how are these goals achieved? The world saves through power, through competition, through the accumulation of strength and prestige. But we have already seen that Jesus, also committed to the advancement of a society, held the people themselves to be the prime value; and love of those neighbors, those people, is the most important thing and is the way to bring in the kingdom. There is a serious conflict here. In the case of the world and society, competition and power are the key; in the kingdom of God being loving or just being a faithful human being is all that is required. The chief ingredient to obeying God is love, as Jesus made very clear.

The minister, be he or she preacher or priest, is charged with those same values. If some of us are set aside, it is not because we are more righteous or have more access to God's presence, but because we have the gift to challenge the standards of the world and to point the way for all the people of God, the way to the "promised land." Is there a sign, a rallying thought?

For me, understanding the sabbath points the way to proper

biblical values in a world desperately devoted to the values of work, more influenced by the six days than by the sabbath. There are two traditions of the sabbath in the Scripture: the one found in Exodus (20:8) and the one in Genesis (2:3). The one in Genesis intrigues me, for there is a gradual ascending scale of importance there. In the order of creation those things created later were the higher things, and on the seventh day the Lord rested. Thus, the purpose of creation is not the work of the six days but the rest of the seventh. Heaven will be rest, re-creation, repose, and value for "being" rather than "doing." We shall not be blessed according to our achievements but according to how well we have gently loved one another. In heaven we shall all love one another; it will be our nature. No longer will our name, or our education, or our money, or our monuments determine how we shall be treated or valued. We shall be known by our love, even as the early Christians realized and tried to live out in their daily lives.

You'll remember that in the Old Testament the sabbath is a recurring symbol, a sign of the faithfulness of the people to God. "The land will lie desolate for seventy years, to make up for the Sabbath rest that has not been observed" (2 Chronicles 36:21, TEV).

Further, every seven years was to be the sabbath year, a custom we have carried forward in our universities; it was a time for renewal and refreshment, a time of repose and inventory taking. But that's not all. In the Old Testament every seven sabbath years resulted in the Year of Jubilee—heaven on earth. The slaves were to be freed, the animals released of their burdens; even the land was to lie fallow and rest. It was the idea of the promise, the day of the Lord, the day when everything would be right.

By the time we get to Jesus the purpose of the sabbath had been lost, but not the sabbath itself. Jesus blessed the sabbath symbol further when he defined it as being for persons, not vice versa. The legalists and the shrewish in spirit had made persons subservient to silly sabbath regulations. The sabbath was no longer a symbol of freedom from burden, a sign of joy and hope. It had been distorted until it was itself a tremendous burden.

We Christian people, and especially those who are "ordained" for special sensitivity to the sabbath symbol, must confront our society at every point where life is being squeezed out by the powerful and the competitive whose only goal is achievement of one kind or another.

Sometimes these competitive people are religious. They play the "big is better" game, and strenuous self-help becomes a substitute for faith when, in fact, our salvation, our faith, even our ability to pray, is the free gift of God. People like this can't wait to hear God, can't see God because of the self-induced religion and the dust they are kicking up in their legalistic efforts at do-it-yourself righteousness, bigger churches, and all sorts of good works and deeds.

But sin in our time is often more subtle than such "religious" examples. It is so subtle that it is often not recognized by the churches at all. Not even by those whose business it is to see these things, to know enough about the Bible and theology to know idolatry when they see it, who are ordained and set aside to teach and to warn people about these subtle temptations. Work, it should be clear, is a curse (see Genesis 3:19). Yet workaholics are everywhere, and they justify this denial of God's providential ability by saying it is for their family, for their country, or even for God. When such workaholics retire, when they could spend time contemplating God and his world, loving and serving persons, they are miserable. Some even die because they haven't seen the sabbath symbol; they have not been confronted with the supreme value which is not work and gain but rest and adoration of God.

There is no question that in this sinful world we must work in order to eat. There is no question that there is dutiful and unpleasant work which must be done by us all. Sweat, as the curse in Genesis indicated, will accompany all that we do, even as pain shall follow women in childbirth.

But it is possible to work and to do our duty toward one's employer without making that employer into a god or, more to the point, without killing our spirits and causing us to take our eyes from God and from our neighbor whom we must love in order to be saved or, to put it a better way, whom we shall love if we have felt the grace of God.

Thus, the function of the minister himself or herself and the congregation, as much as is possible this side of heaven, is to confront people, remind people, and engage in leading worship to enable people to know that God is all in all and that the worship of him is a joy forever and ever and, as the old teaching has it, is "the chief end of man."